Michael S Smith
Kitchens and Baths

Michael S Smith
Kitchens and Baths

BY MICHAEL S. SMITH
AND CHRISTINE PITTEL

RIZZOLI
NEW YORK

First published in the United States of America in 2011
by Rizzoli International Publications, Inc.
300 Park Avenue South
New York, NY 10010
www.rizzoliusa.com

2011 2012 2013 2014 / 10 9 8 7 6 5 4 3 2 1

Distributed in the U.S. trade by Random House, New York

Printed in China

ISBN-13: 978-0-8478-3677-2

Library of Congress Catalog Control Number: 2011927897

Art Direction: Doug Turshen with Steve Turner

TABLE OF CONTENTS

INTRODUCTION

When I'm watching a movie like *Gosford Park* or *Sabrina* or the latest English-country-house saga, I can't wait for the camera to move out of the drawing room and into the back-of-the-house spaces. That's because what I really want to see are the kitchens and the baths.

They share the distinction of being the places where water comes into a house, and they may also be the most expensive and labor-intensive rooms to build. But besides having plumbing in common, they are opposites—the most public and the most private zones of a house. People gather in a kitchen; they retreat to a bath to be alone . . . or alone together.

In a way, they're the most difficult rooms to do. When I approach a kitchen, I feel like Baron Haussmann faced with the task of redesigning Paris. Figuring out the layout—sink, refrigerator, and stove; upper and lower cabinets and work surfaces; water, electricity, and gas—is like planning a miniature city. There are certain givens, but you want to put them together in a way that feels fresh. And on some level, if you can design a kitchen cabinet, you can design a skyscraper. Sometimes I'll take a detail from a door or a mantel and repeat it on the cabinets. To me, they're a microcosm of all the architecture in a house.

It's an interesting challenge—how do you create a sense of a particular time and place when you're stuck with all these modern appliances? Function is the driving force, yet you can't forget comfort as well. People want to be able to live in their kitchens, so you have to make room for family and friends. The designer becomes a kind of social engineer, planning spaces that encourage this convivial notion of family life. And often, an element of wishful thinking kicks in—the illusion that we're suddenly going to start baking bread or rolling out pastry dough on that lovely marble-topped counter.

If the kitchen is task-oriented, the bathroom is where we go to relax and leave the world behind—or at least that's the fantasy. It's often the most aspirational space in the house, the room that reflects a vision of who we would like to be. In the morning, people compose themselves here before they go out into the world. And then at night, it becomes more of a dream state. Here we are cleansed, shedding all vestiges of the day and stepping out of one life into another. It's a very personal space, a projection of our innermost self and our deepest desires.

When you're doing a house or an apartment, these are the rooms where you should indulge yourself. So I've gathered up some examples that might give you some ideas and help you along. We've divided them up according to place rather than style, because it turns out that most rooms are rather hard to define in a word or two . . . just like most people.

BEACH

MALIBU, CALIFORNIA

Twelve acres on a cliff overlooking the ocean in Malibu—it was a once-in-a-lifetime piece of property. The only problem was the house that came with it. Built in the 1980s, it was huge—about 19,000 square feet—and very grand, designed for formal entertaining with swaths of fabric draped across the windows and chandeliers all over the place. My clients weren't sure—it was definitely not their taste—and strict local laws limited how much of the structure itself could be changed. Was it salvageable?

Definitely. I looked at it and immediately knew what it should be: a Palladian villa. It already had the scale. Now what we needed was simplicity. Architect Oscar Shamamian and I took it apart like a puzzle and remade it, following Palladio's principles of proportion and symmetry. We moved walls and rearranged doorways to create strong axes. We opened it up to the ocean light and the breeze. I wanted loftlike rooms with soaring ceilings that were so perfect in their proportions that they looked quite beautiful empty.

As in a sixteenth-century Palladian villa, the materials are raw yet refined. The entire ground floor is paved in *pietra serena*, the stones of Florence. Walls are made of Venetian plaster, which has depth and texture and seems to echo the colors of the sand on the beach.

You can see the simple, monumental quality of the redesigned house in the columns. This loggia overlooking the Pacific is a glorious spot for dining, and it comes equipped with a fireplace to take the chill off those cool summer nights.

I'm interested in the pull of opposites—ancient and
modern, straight and curved, rough and refined.

Palladio was the starting point, but nothing I do is quite that easy to define. There are always various images and ideas ricocheting around in my brain. In this house, Palladio and a kind of Belgian minimalism fused into this concept of sixteenth-century loft living. And then it somehow merged with Japanese feudal palaces—someone had given me a book, and I couldn't get those pictures out of my head—and then that blended with northern European castles to arrive at this kitchen with stone shelves, stainless steel cabinets, and a Japanese *tansu* chest.

The forms are simple and powerful. The island is a slab of walnut with straight, minimal lines. It has a solid, weighty quality, which gives it a certain gravitas. Then above it are these vaporous floating lights—super-interesting—made of cotton cloth stretched over thin strips of wood. They once hung in a Japanese department store. And then those circles are echoed in the circle incised on the hood over the range. A circle is a strong shape and a powerful symbol, although I wasn't thinking of anything in particular when I chose it. It's not meant to represent the rising sun, for example, although you can read into it anything you like. For me, it's all about the geometry. It's a circle in a square.

The range is a BlueStar, which is about as close to a commercial range as you can get for a home. It has one exceptionally hot and extremely fast burner, and it will light up the eyes of any good chef. The cabinets next to it on that wall are made of stainless steel to continue the metallic line.

In this kitchen, there's a subliminal contest going on between the wood and the stainless steel. Which is going to dominate? I wanted a balance. The wood keeps the stainless steel from becoming too cold, and the stainless steel keeps the wood from becoming too cloying.

It's fascinating to me how wood has a way of civilizing a space. It makes a kitchen feel more genteel, yet it also has this intrinsic power that enables it to challenge the stainless steel. You don't feel that this is an industrial kitchen. The wood has domesticated the space.

I love how the textures play off one another—the Lagos Azul limestone counters and backsplash against the Venetian plaster walls, the brushed stainless steel against the dark wood. I deliberately limited the palette to keep it pure and simple. The whole room is actually made up of only four materials—wood, plaster, steel, and stone. Yet you don't get tired of them because they're all very tactile. The wood is burnished and smooth. The stone and the plaster are a little more raw and earthy. Even the stainless steel attracts your hand because it's brushed, which gives it a softer quality, almost a patina. That balance of cool and warm elements makes the room very comfortable to be in. It's modern, but not cold.

It's *Shogun* in Malibu, although there's very little here that's overtly Japanese—just the lamps and the collection of flower-arranging baskets on the stone shelves. I think the impression comes more from the purity of the lines. The island is a simple rectilinear form combined with simple rectilinear stools from BDDW that are made with thick saddle leather. The hanging lights are large enough to establish their own center of gravity. They give the room a second ceiling in a way, and make it feel more intimate.
FOLLOWING SPREAD: I wanted a contemporary version of a traditional gooseneck faucet and designed these for Kallista as part of my Town line. They're in a brushed nickel finish, which always looks elegant to me. The two wall ovens are massed into a composition that incorporates a vent, so the three elements become a sleek stainless steel column that corresponds to the height of the doors.

ABOVE: One side of the island is fitted with stainless steel cabinets. The sink is set into a slab of Lagos Azul limestone so you don't have the sink right next to wood, which always makes me a little nervous. A refrigerator is hidden within the storage wall. OPPOSITE: I chose those early nineteenth-century English bobbin chairs for the breakfast room because I liked their severe, sculptural shape. They look almost feudal. The English lantern has equally strong lines.

A separate pantry is a very convenient luxury,
especially when the owners are giving a large party.
It doubles the storage space as well as the work area.

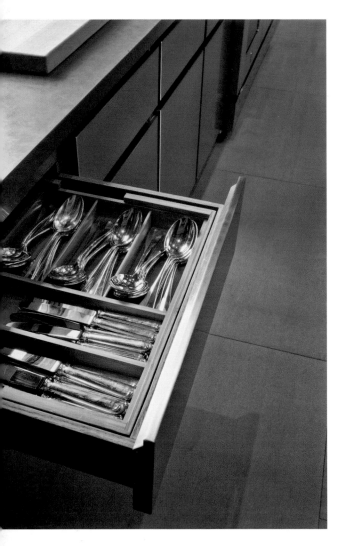

A kitchen in a house this size needs to have a split personality. It should be equally comfortable for a family or an army of caterers. When the family is home alone, they can all gather round the island and talk and cook together. Everything they need to make and serve a meal is in this one room.

Then, when they're throwing a party, the separate pantry next door comes into play. It's equipped like a duplicate kitchen, with plenty of workspace and another sink and more refrigeration. Each of the rooms is configured with separate zones for prep and cooking and plating food, so that many people can work here without getting in one another's way.

When you're designing a kitchen, decide what you're going to be doing in each area and that will determine where you place the appliances. You'll want dishwashers near the sink, landing space—in other words, countertops—beside the sink and the refrigerator and the stove. It doesn't make sense to put a stove next to a wall, or a cold refrigerator next to a hot stove. It's always pleasant to have a window over the sink. And don't forget a pullout drawer for trash, with recycling bins.

ABOVE: Drawer inserts make it easy to organize the contents. OPPOSITE: A separate pantry is equipped with a stainless steel storage wall and a Sub-Zero PRO 48 refrigerator.

Slow down. Put everything out of your mind and take a long bath on a lazy afternoon.

When you walk through the front door of this house, I wanted you to feel as if a weight has been lifted off your shoulders. Inside, everything is calm, peaceful, serene. The atmosphere is light and airy. You have room to breathe. The master bathrooms—one for the wife and one for the husband—embody this notion of tranquility.

For her, I had this image of a lady in a tower. It could be in a villa of the Veneto, or there are even suggestions of a Roman bath in a vaulted room, lit only by oil lamps. There is a simplicity here that suggests another time and place. The space is classically composed with that arching ceiling, the travertine floor, and the tub silhouetted against the window. When you make a tub the centerpiece of a room, it's a very powerful gesture. Even if you're not in it, I think you feel an immediate sense of relaxation. It quiets the room.

There's something innately romantic about soaking in warm water while looking out at the ocean. I kept the rest of the room relatively subdued, so as not to distract from the view. The walls are a sand-colored Venetian plaster, and the curtains are a beige-and-blush Fortuny cotton that looks as if it belongs in an Italian palazzo. Venetian plaster is a centuries-old technique, and Fortuny fabric has been made in exactly the same way for generations. Each has a certain patina that helps soften the space.

On the other side of the room is a shower lined in Egyptian onyx, book-matched so the pattern on adjoining slabs forms a mirror image. The onyx gives the shower—a very modern convenience—an antique quality. The furniture follows through with the same illusion. I copied a seventeenth-century English table for the vanity. I wanted it to look as if you had taken a piece of old family furniture and modified it to hold a sink. The dressing table copies the same form and is paired with a mirror that swings open on either end, to hold makeup and toiletries yet keep them out of sight. If you build in enough storage space, you can get rid of all the clutter and keep the surfaces clean, which also contributes to the feeling of serenity.

An interesting light fixture can do a lot to create mood. This chandelier is Egyptian, with little glass vases hung on chains in a way that looks positively ancient. But then the swing-arm lamps look as if they could be French, from the 1940s. And the chair at the dressing table is Italian, with neoclassical lines. It's a very European blend of furnishings, as if these pieces had been collected over generations by the family who lives in this house. The time frame blurs.

This room is devoted to bathing, so it makes perfect sense to center it on the Mercer tub by Urban Archaeology, with Etoile fixtures by Waterworks. The curtains at the window feel almost like curtains on a stage, with a very thin bamboo shade to veil the sunlight. The travertine on the floor and the wainscot looks like something you would find at the beach, polished by the waves. A Chinese porcelain garden stool is there to hold a drink. There's something wonderful about wrapping yourself in a warm towel, so we installed a heated towel rack.

There is a warmth to
all the stone we chose,
from the onyx to the
travertine, and the
colors and textures of
the furnishings pick
up the same tones.
The neoclassical
Italian chair is covered
in antique velvet.
A Turkish rug adds
more softness.

The paneling is made of lime-washed oak and cut to look like rusticated stone, so you get the idea of old stone walls but with this lovely, unexpected warmth.

If you were a descendant of the Medici family and had decamped from Florence to your villa in the countryside for the summer, this is where you would shave in the morning. I'll admit it bears some resemblance to a room in the Greek and Roman wing of a museum, with that extraordinary Byzantine mosaic set into the floor, but the difference is that you actually get to live here.

This bathroom was designed for the husband, and it has a strong masculine sensibility, with oak paneling on the walls and dark wood furniture. It's a large, beautifully detailed space with ceilings that are probably twelve feet high. Yet you never feel overwhelmed, because architect Oscar Shamamian did such a great job of keeping the rooms in this house on a human scale while still giving them those soaring classical proportions. When you walk in, you feel uplifted.

I loved that heroic quality and did not want to muck it up with too much furniture. The idea was to keep it spare, as those Palladian villas actually were in their time. I want you to see the beautiful bones of the room—the classical cornices and the majestic door surrounds and the stately paneling—and then your eye should alight on the few carefully chosen pieces of furniture. There's an English table with a specimen marble top in the center of the room. It has a simple shape, but the richly patterned marble conveys a subtle sense of luxury.

Old master oil paintings hang on the walls, but between them is a more unexpected piece—an early nineteenth-century Chinese cabinet that once again has very simple lines yet great presence. What is it doing here? It could be the souvenir of some ancestor's round-the-world trip or simply the result of a good eye on a shopping expedition. But it brings another flavor into the room and adds to the exotic mix of cultures.

At first glance, you could almost miss the actual bathroom fittings. The vanity simply looks like another piece of furniture. The Derbyshire stone on top is from England, and it's an earthy reddish brown—just one of the many shades of brown in the room. I like a monochromatic room. Visually, it has great strength, and a tone-on-tone palette also turns out to be very restful, which suits a bathroom.

I think you want a sense of peace, and the architecture of a room can help you achieve it. All those straight, rectilinear lines on the paneling create a sense of order. It feels very solid and rational. The shapes of the panels and the way they are staggered remind me of stone. So you have this wonderful fusion of an agrarian and a modern ideal—the rusticated stone building that evolved into those glorious Palladian villas, now reimagined for a contemporary way of life.

I like to mix messages. In a relatively formal room with Fortuny curtains in the Persepolis pattern hanging at the windows, there's something very disarming—and practical—about this simple, basic vanity with its open shelves. Wicker baskets by Palecek hold towels and add a rustic note. Everything you touch is beautiful—the faucet handles are accented with wood. The Derbyshire stone I chose for the countertop is a rich brown and has all these intriguing prehistoric fossils trapped inside it. PREVIOUS SPREAD: The light fixtures, with their hanging bronze bowls, have that early Roman or Etruscan look and accentuate the antique aspect of the room. I also like the fact that you don't see the source of the light; all you get is the glow. The Byzantine mosaic on the floor dates back to the fourth century B.C., and yet look at the pattern. It could almost be modern.

This house has a Silk Road sensibility. The objects come from all sorts of countries—many of them along that famous trade route.

One of the things that makes the modern age great (and a little startling) is that we're all so connected. Communication is instantaneous. As a result, no idea or concept or art object is totally pure. We all influence one another. That's been going on for a long time, and the process has merely sped up today.

History is all about hybrids. Palladio's architectural concept of an Italian villa gets reworked by John Vanbrugh and Nicholas Hawksmoor at Castle Howard in England and then winds up inspiring Drayton Hall, a plantation house in South Carolina. One culture has always left its mark on another, either through trade or conquest or immigration, or simply through the power of a good idea.

And that mix of cultures and the objects they produce makes a room more interesting. In a guest bathroom, a rare dark green English marble tops a vanity and adds a luxurious touch to a tub-and-shower combination. Let me walk you through the rest of the furnishings, and you'll see that they constitute a mini world tour. There's a Chinese ancestor portrait hanging above a rack of French and Turkish towels. The rolling cart by the tub is Indian, made of ebonized wood and accented with ivory roundels. An early Georgian chair from England has a cushion covered in Mali Stripe, a fabric from my own line. It's based on an old African fabric that I found. Now I make my own version, with real indigo dye, in Guatemala. The matchstick shades at the window are Japanese, and the straw-and-leather mat on the floor is from Marrakech. Each object brings a whiff of another place and a different aesthetic, making this a very well-traveled room.

ABOVE: Prints of Karnak in Egypt hang in another guest bathroom, next to an Italian deco mirror. I bought it because I loved that blue glass frame. The Waterworks faucet was custom-made for us in a bronze finish. OPPOSITE: Another ancient-looking light fixture, the Naples chandelier from my Jasper collection, takes you back in time. The toilet is from my Loft collection for Kallista. The floor is made of reclaimed brown oak—just waxed, no urethane—which keeps it looking old and smoky.

MALIBU, CALIFORNIA

A beach house doesn't have to be white canvas slipcovers and sisal rugs. Here, I was after that sense of calmness and simplicity that always seems to suit a house by the ocean, but I wanted to get to it in a different way, to find another flavor.

This was a new house, but you'd never know it—it was very thoughtfully built in the kind of classic Shingle Style that looks as if it has been around forever. The architecture made it feel very East Coast to me, as if we could be on Nantucket or Martha's Vineyard in some old sea captain's home. Once I had that picture in my head, I could imagine him voyaging around the world and bringing back some of the more exotic pieces—like that magnificent seventeenth-century Dutch cupboard, the English dining table, and the Chinese lanterns. It's a little unexpected to see all that dark wood in this ethereal California light, but I like it. It establishes a sense of history and also anchors the space, giving you something solid to hang on to during those gray days at the beach when the air is a cloud of mist.

The adjacent living room is done in paler, watery colors, which makes it even more interesting to have this strong dark note. The contrast prevents your eye from getting bored. And I was careful to keep this dining area very spare, with only the table, the Dutch cupboard, and the lantern. When each piece has such presence, you don't really need any more. Against the cream-colored walls, the antiques—with all their finely carved details—register as elegant, not heavy. When you sit down to breakfast here, you feel as if you're part of a long tradition, surrounded by furnishings that have meant something to this family for a very long time.

Handsome proportions, impeccable detailing—that's what drew me to that Dutch cabinet, which dates back to 1650 and is made of ebony and palisander. The English table, which was made around 1850, shows a similar play of dark and light wood, with ebony accents on the pollard oak. But what really makes this room linger in your memory is that lantern. The more predictable choice would have been a chandelier. But this is a beach house, and you would be more likely to have a lantern because it's more casual, and the candles wouldn't get blown out in the wind. So it fits the story, and it's also got that huge, crazy scale, which gives it even more impact. This is a reproduction of a late eighteenth-century Strawberry Hill Gothic chinoiserie lantern from a shop in London called Soane. The James chairs are from my own line. I took a country Chippendale form and kind of pumped it up to make it a little more modern and graphic, so the chairs can hold their own against all these other strong shapes.

You still see a few old cottages along the beach in Malibu, and I wanted to instill this place with something of their simple, unaffected charm.

The next question was, what should an old sea captain's kitchen look like?

Nothing fussy. No little steering wheels or fishnets or other nautical memorabilia on the walls. I decided it would be as plain and simple as the landscape outside. I wanted the kitchen to be the colors of sea and sand, so we painted the walls a kind of faded blue-green and the cabinets a pale khaki. Very pretty. There's a lot of gray in the light in Malibu on a June morning, and I thought the blue would pull the room together and make you feel more cozy, as if you had wrapped yourself in a soft shawl.

I decided the equipment should be basic as well—an old-fashioned farmhouse sink, gooseneck faucet, open shelves. A weathered mahogany on the countertops helps give it that cottagey feel. And then the island takes you somewhere else. It looks more like a table, and the detailing is straight out of the Aesthetic Movement—that late nineteenth-century style popularized by William Morris. It featured all sorts of natural imagery of birds and flowers and was strongly influenced by Japanese wood-block prints, which were exhibited for the first time in England in 1885. The wooden furniture was usually made in ebonized black and we did that here, so the dark island vaguely recalls the dark woods in the dining room. Then the stools are painted a verdigris green, which doesn't really go with anything at all. The idea is that you had these pieces for years and just put them together. They relate to each other but they don't match, which creates a casual effect.

And then those playful Chinese lanterns come as a complete surprise. What are they doing here? Well, they could be the spoils of another voyage. And they're Asian, so there's a kind of connection to the Aesthetic Movement. But really, I just thought they looked wonderful, and that's why they're here.

OPPOSITE: The kitchen is done in muted blues and taupes that could have come straight out of the view from the deck. The paint on the walls is Farrow & Ball's Blue Gray, and the cabinets are done in Pratt & Lambert's Silver Blond. I designed the island and had it topped with charcoal-colored stone. The Newport bar stool is by Charles Fradin. The mid-nineteenth-century Chinese lanterns are from the Shanxi province and were found at Kim3 International Furnishings. ABOVE: The boundless ocean view from the deck.

Every room deserves one dramatic element, and in the master bath it's that huge eccentric mirror. I couldn't resist it. The bubbles reminded me of the ocean.

The bathroom has white wainscoting with pale blue paint above, and I could have left it at that—classic, comfortable, appealing. But it went into a whole other dimension once I added that mirror. The size is unexpected, and the shape is almost surreal. It looks a bit like a pocket watch up there on the wall. Suddenly the room acquired a sense of humor. The tub, which is also big, started to look like one of those spinning-teacup rides at an amusement park. Now, I admit, probably no one else is going to see it that way, but it made the room feel a lot more fun.

It was a large room, and if I have the square footage, I like to bring in a chair. Here a chaise is even better, because you can put your feet up and relax after a bath, or even read a bit in that lovely corner overlooking the ocean. I covered the chaise in a multicolored print that has a storybook quality, very medieval King Arthur. Then there's an Indian étagère stacked with towels and a Moroccan side table where you could set down a drink. So you have all these exotic elements that push this simple beach house in unexpected directions.

ABOVE: How many bathrooms would you actually want to sit and read in? This is one where the impulse is not so far-fetched, because it's furnished like a room with a chaise and a lamp, so you would even have enough light to finish your book late at night. The ebonized table against the wall brings back that dark note that runs throughout the house. OPPOSITE: The iron-framed mirror from JF Chen is the largest circle in a composition of circles that also includes the iron sconces. The walls are painted in Pratt & Lambert's Coos Bay.

LAGUNA BEACH, CALIFORNIA

In an Italianate house, inspired by the centuries-old villas the client had seen along the Amalfi coast, and built with stone and stucco and massive beams, what do you do about the kitchen? There is no such thing as a seventeenth-century Italian refrigerator or a Tuscan microwave . . . thank God. So how can you be true to the spirit of the house and still have a state-of-the-art kitchen?

The architect, Bob White, got it right. He worked from the premise that this was an old agrarian building that had been redone, and he placed various modern interventions against the "historical" shell. Factory-style steel windows and doors are set into old-fashioned Venetian plaster walls, and the juxtaposition of new and old takes the kitchen out of its time warp and prevents it from looking like Disneyland. The island appears to be a hefty antique table that has been adapted to this new use, with a copper prep sink dropped in. And there's no attempt to hide the stainless steel dishwashers or refrigerator. All of these materials have a tactile quality. They invite you to run your fingers over them, and the counterpoint between the cool, industrial stainless and the warm wood keeps the whole thing from getting too heavy. The faucet on the main sink looks very high-tech. It's equipped with an industrial-size hose, and the sink itself is the size of an animal trough. Yet it's carved out of elegant Carrara marble. So you've also got this lovely blur between the rustic and the refined going on.

The ceiling is an area that's often forgotten in a kitchen, but here the wood planks and beams connote age and give the room a wonderful cozy quality. And the floor, made of reclaimed Dalle de Bourgogne stone from Exquisite Surfaces, makes the room feel as if it has been here forever.

Notice the handsome turned leg on the corner of the island and how the sink looks like it has been carved out of a solid block of marble. Bob White did a beautiful job on those. There are no veneers on the wood here. Everything feels solid and substantial and simple. With that industrial-size faucet, you could practically hose down that stone floor. Upper cabinets would look too suburban, so we did open shelves, which conveniently allow you to see everything at a glance.

Pendant lights over an island are a great opportunity to restate a theme. I chose these fixtures by Alison Berger because they embody the fusion of old and new. She takes contemporary glass and gives it another dimension. I look at those lights and think of pre-Renaissance alchemy, the romance of early science. The sixty-inch Château range by La Cornue is the Rolls-Royce of kitchen appliances, and looks regal, crowned with a coordinating hood. A huge slab of Carrara marble serves as a splendid backsplash. So beautiful, it's almost like a painting to me. FOLLOWING SPREAD: The living room is open to the kitchen, which makes this monumental room—with stone walls and a baronial fireplace—feel more relaxed and casual.

What could be more romantic than an old-fashioned French copper tub in a tower?

The master bath is high up in a tower, with windows that wrap a corner and bathe the tub in light. It's a bateau tub made of copper, a metal that automatically suggests warmth, and as you step into it you feel as if you've stepped into another era. But where are we? The room almost suggests a cloister, with that lofty wooden ceiling and marble floor. You can't quite pin down the style. There's a Marco Polo aspect to the furnishings, as if various family members went off to see the world and came home laden with treasures. Antique furniture, like the turn-of-the-century Indian cabinet inlaid with bone, can give so much to a space. Antiques tell a story. Built-ins may be practical, but they just don't have the history or the patina. And this room is all about patina, the kind you get when you have natural materials that are lovingly crafted. That's really all you need, especially if you have this celestial light. Curtains would have been too cumbersome, so I just hung thin matchstick blinds, with a color like smoked wood, which we have made in Japan. In a weird way, I think this is one of the most successful rooms in the house. All those stories give it a real sense of mystery and romance.

ABOVE: The blue chandelier comes out of nowhere, but who cares? There is something about Venetian glass that is always magical. A Turkish rug warms the marble floor. OPPOSITE: The chair looks Chinese at first glance, but it's actually an Italian antique—a perfect illustration of the power of an iconic shape and the influence of one culture on another. The Medicis copper tub is by Herbeau, and the faucet and hand spray are by Waterworks.

LAGUNA BEACH, CALIFORNIA

Just steps from the sand, this great little beach bungalow is the perfect getaway. It's refreshingly simple, with one big room that functions as living room, dining room, and kitchen, two small bedrooms, and a large courtyard off the back where you can soak up the sun. It's easy to move from indoors to out, and because the living area is very open, there's almost no sense of boundaries. It's like living in a loft.

I grew up in the area, and I appreciate the charm of these houses. The whole point is to keep it simple. You don't want to gussy it up. But on the other hand, if you're too modest, you risk being taken for granted. So I decided on one bold gesture. I painted the floor, but not in the classic beach-house white. Instead, I chose a bright apple green.

It cheers you up to walk into the kitchen in the morning and make yourself a cup of coffee and see that green floor. Sunlight pours in and reflects off the surface. There's a sheen and a life to it. It's like a substitute lawn. The enamel deck paint is durable. You can wash it repeatedly. And it gives you that crisp, shipshape boat vibe. I like the way it sets off the sleek but simple rectangular kitchen table. Somehow, that table manages to be modern and traditional at the same time. It works with both the stainless steel Sub-Zero and the old-fashioned painted cabinets.

We did something a little different with the island. It still has the typical white marble top and functions as the main prep area. But then it grew and morphed into a piece of furniture that actually works as an architectural divider, separating the kitchen from the living room. So it has a split personality, with kitchen things stored on the kitchen side and a TV and stereo behind the doors on the living room side. It's a big piece, but because it's painted white, it seems more self-effacing. The eye doesn't get stopped by it. You register that it's there, but then you move on to other details in the room, like the Venetian mirror over the fireplace or the light streaming in through the windows.

The house can expand or contract, depending on what you need. You could invite twenty-five people for dinner, use the island and the kitchen table as a buffet, and eat outside in the courtyard. Or two people could sit alone by the fire and feel very cozy. The room becomes very intimate. The open plan is infinitely flexible and lets you experience it in different ways.

I designed the kitchen table, with its square chrome legs and dark wooden top. It's a play on an industrial idea, kind of like a modern version of a factory piece. The chrome relates to the stove and has a utilitarian quality, but then it also works as a wonderful dining table because of the warmth of the wood. The Eames chairs surrounding it are comfortable but lean. They say modern and California, but then I added my own twist by putting pony-skin covers on them. The Holophane lights define the dining area, and when you turn them on and leave the rest of the room dim, you could forget you're dining in the kitchen. With very little adjustment, it becomes an elegant room.

The apple green–painted floor unifies the space, but then the large island subtly divides it into kitchen and living area. Those doors in the center open to reveal a TV. You could eat on the coffee table in front of it, if you like. All the furnishings are casual. There are no rules here. Relax.

The bedroom is open to the bathroom, which makes both rooms feel larger. It's also more sensual. You can lie in bed and talk to your mate as she takes a shower.

The palette is very restful. The same white marble that was on the kitchen island is on the vanity. It makes sense in a small house to repeat the same materials. It creates a nice continuity. The Palladian window above the sink captures more natural light and adds classical elegance to a small space. But this bathroom does not feel small, and that's predominantly because of the floor-to-ceiling window in the shower. You can open the whole thing and still have privacy, because it looks out on a private courtyard. It's almost like showering in the open air, and it connects you, once again, to nature. And isn't that what we all want in a beach house?

ABOVE LEFT: The Shaker-style canopy bed adds a little architecture to a plain room and faces the focal point of the bath—the Palladian window. ABOVE RIGHT: The Venetian chandelier may be a little indulgent, but it works because of its clarity. It almost disappears. OPPOSITE: The relatively elaborate shower system makes this simple bathroom feel like a fine hotel. The bronze windows have a nice weight and can stand up to the moisture. I like the old-fashioned look of the Ann-Morris swing-arm lights, and they can be dimmed for atmosphere or brightened when you need to see what you're doing.

MALIBU, CALIFORNIA

You know that great feeling you get when you're on vacation? You're relaxed, open to adventure, and happy to be in some exotic place. Well, architect Oscar Shamamian and I wanted to take that feeling and incorporate it into this house.

I'd describe it as a cross between an Asian tea plantation during the British Colonial era and one of those amazing Aman resort hotels in Bali or Sri Lanka. It's built on various levels that step down a hillside overlooking the ocean, and the doors to the terrace and the pool slide back into the walls so they seem to vanish. It feels as if you're outdoors even when you're indoors in these big, breezy rooms. The kitchen is part of a large family room, and it had to be extra-practical since these clients like to cook and entertain. But at the same time, I wanted it to have some of the sultry sensuality of the tropics.

Color is a shortcut to mood. That blue-green on the walls and the cabinets is almost a peacock blue, a color that conjures up those exotic birds or the deep blue waters of the Caribbean. It's lush and romantic and unexpected. The Lagos Azul limestone on the countertops has the dark gray smoothness of wet river stones. Then the island is topped with deep brown mahogany that brings in a bit of the rain forest. It's a strong palette, but you need something strong next to the family room. The furniture there is covered in fabrics by John Robshaw and dyed with real indigo. The blues are so rich and intense that they feel almost tribal. I added a touch of red on the barstools and on the quilt tossed over the sofa. It's equally vibrant and somehow warms up the room.

I modeled the barstools after a chair I saw in Morocco. The dining room chairs are another version of the same thought. They're low and relaxed, like something you might see in Rangoon at an old British officers' club. The fretwork and the carving suggest the touch of the hand, and for me that carries a lot of charm.

Give me a ceiling fan and I'm suddenly in the Raffles Hotel, drinking a Singapore Sling and living out my Somerset Maugham fantasy. I lined the ceiling with grass cloth to make it feel more tropical. This is the place where everyone likes to sit, and the fact that it's open to the kitchen means that the host and the hostess are part of the party, even when they're preparing the meal.

A fireplace in a dining room is a great asset, and I covered the ceiling with white-gold leaf to add to the glow. The copper-and-glass lantern is British, and I found it at Ann-Morris Antiques. The painting is by Nancy Lorenz.

There's something innately elegant about white marble and dark mahogany. It's classic, understated, and luxurious, and it's all part of my British Colonial fantasy.

Step into this room, and it's better than an airplane ticket. It represents the easiest way to travel, because you immediately feel as if you're in some exotic place in a more glamorous era, and you never even have to leave home. For me, it's part Raffles Hotel and part Orient Express. The sconces by the mirrors, with their frosted glass and heavy silver fittings, look art deco. And there's a finely carved bullnose edge on the marble, which also takes me right back to the 1930s.

The mahogany cabinetry is impeccably done. I like the way the tub is encased in woodwork. It sits in a bay, and the vanity sits in a bay. The symmetries make the bathroom feel very organized and planned out.

The finish on the fixtures is a brushed silver, just like the sconces. It actually has some real silver in it, which gives it a lovely soft quality. When you touch a handle, it feels like a piece of jewelry. The finish on a faucet is something that people often forget to specify, not realizing that they have a choice. It may seem like an insignificant thing, but the difference between chrome, nickel, brass, bronze, silver, or gold affects the whole nature of a bathroom. A brushed finish is more practical than a polished finish, because it is less likely to show fingerprints or water spots.

Every element in this bathroom is something you want to touch. The marble has a beautiful creamy quality. It doesn't seem flat, because the veins and swirls in the stone give it some dimension. It reminds me of watered silk. I happen to think there's something very romantic about hanging lights, especially when they're made of cloudy glass. I bought this one at Charles Edwards in London. The stepped shape echoes the sconces, which are a redo by JF Chen of a French original. I love the sense of history these fixtures bring to the room. They're redolent of a certain time, yet timeless.

The floor is made of mahogany inset with marble, like a kind of stone carpet. A chic little African drum holds towels close by. The tub, sink, and fixtures are all from my Town collection for Kallista. If you look in the side mirror, you'll see a reflection of the TV—a twenty-first-century necessity.

PACIFIC PALISADES, CALIFORNIA

This house was originally designed for Ronald Colman by the architect Cliff May, who is known as the father of the California ranch house—those low-slung, wide-open houses where every room has some connection to the outdoors. When I first saw it, someone had painted the rooms in intense colors like bright turquoise and shocking pink. We toned it down with a quiet but rich palette that brought out the good bones of the architecture.

The interesting thing about the California ranch house is that it's a twentieth-century interpretation of a much earlier style—the Spanish hacienda. People moving to California from back east fused New England architecture with local building methods to create this hybrid that existed only in the West.

You can see this fusion in these his-and-hers bathrooms. The wainscoting on the walls feels very New England, but the texture and color of the plaster above it is more California. The husband's bathroom is beautifully simple in taupes and creams. It's also the perfect illustration of how one piece of furniture can inflect a room. That antique chair, which feels like a more rustic version of a William Morris design, takes the room into the Arts & Crafts period.

In the wife's bathroom, the equivalent piece is that mirrored dressing table, which adds a little 1940s Hollywood glamour. Her furnishings are eclectic: the Moroccan table, the French mirror. Each piece has its own personality, very different from one another, and you wouldn't expect to see them in the same room. But that free-for-all mix conveys an idea of her personality. Clearly, she's a free spirit who does exactly what she wants to do and doesn't feel the need to abide by any rules.

Both rooms have reclaimed oak floors. I think there is something luxurious about a wood floor in a bathroom. It's quiet, solid, and it has this lovely warmth to it—much nicer than cold, hard tile, especially when your feet are bare. And it says old-fashioned and comfortable to me. I'll add an antique rug to bring in another layer, some texture, and a little pattern. But the colors are usually soft and worn. In these rooms, the rugs become part of the background. They're not the first things you notice. Yet they contribute to the mood. I love the way they add patina and give a room a sense of history.

The color and texture of the walls in this bathroom remind me of adobe, in that soft tortilla color. There's nothing fancy here. Towels are simply hung on hooks. But the shower is pure pleasure, equipped with everything you could want, including a rain showerhead. Niches are built into the wall to hold shampoos and conditioners within reach. And it has a window, which makes the stall feel less confined. You can open the window and feel the summer breeze as you scrub down.

This bathroom has all the creature comforts, but its delights are subtle. The tub is built for soaking, with a languid curve that tempts you to lie back. The faucets are plated with sterling silver, which is something you might not even notice until you touch them, and it gives a beautifully soft and rich look. Both the tub and the fixtures are from my Town collection for Kallista. The linen curtains and shades at the window almost blend into the color of the walls and frame a view of venerable oaks.

OAHU, HAWAII

Hawaii in the 1930s was a very simple place, as you can see in this modest bungalow from that period. It was probably designed by the architect Charles W. Dickey, who grew up on the island and appreciated the vernacular plantation style, then enriched it with elements of Japanese architecture and California Mission style.

The house has a long, low, almost Asian roof and a minimum of walls to take advantage of the trade winds to cool the interiors. Broad projecting eaves shelter the rooms from the sun and protect them from passing showers, so there's no need to rush to close the doors every time it rains. Anything not indigenous to the island had to be shipped in, so you don't see a lot of extraneous furnishings in these houses. Materials had to be able to survive the salt air and the humidity, so the interiors were much more utilitarian than you might think.

I wanted to respect that sense of plainness—almost a kind of innocence—when I redid this kitchen. Concrete is a simple material that you see in many of these old houses, and it was the logical choice for the kitchen floor. I've always been captivated by it. There's that intriguing dichotomy—it's hard, yet somehow soft. It's considered a lowly material, and yet it can have a certain kind of velvety richness. We mixed in some green and blue pigment to add patches of color and poured it over the floor. Then we scored it with lines to create a subtle pattern. A vintage Hawaiian colonial pedestal table, painted white to clean it up and pull it into the present, is centered on the central square.

I paired the table with vintage aluminum chairs that look as if they could have come out of some Pearl Harbor–era naval base. They're extremely practical, with plain, simple lines, and you wouldn't expect to see them next to this traditionally carved table. But now this breakfast nook, which could have been completely innocuous, is suddenly interesting. Your eye is caught by the contrast and stops for a minute, trying to figure out what's going on.

The rest of the room is refreshingly artless—vertical-plank walls painted white, matchstick blinds, an old wooden worktable. It all looks as if it has been there forever. There's no hint that a decorator even touched it. It's very underdone. And that allows the essence of the island to emerge. If I'm going to fly all the way to Hawaii, I want to feel like I'm in Hawaii when I get there. I don't want the kind of generic "tropical resort" decorating that you could see in umpteen high-rise hotels on the ocean. The whole point is to get away from it all.

In this house, you have the garden on one side and the ocean on the other. Louvered shutters can be slid across the door to block out the sun while they let in the breeze. Architect Nancy Peacock worked on the restoration of the house. FOLLOWING SPREAD: You can conjure up an era with one small detail, like those blue-green glass knobs on the cabinets that evoke the 1930s. The countertops are made of terrazzo, another material that was popular during that time. They're embedded with chunks of blue-green glass that pick up the same colors.

When I saw that vintage bamboo table with the wedge-shaped seats, I thought it would be a great place to play games. And the children could sit down and have a meal there.

In this bathroom, you have a choice of showering indoors or out. It opens to a private courtyard with an outdoor shower—very tempting on a sultry day and convenient after a morning at the beach, to wash the sand away. The door stays open most of the time because there's rarely a reason to close it.

This kind of permeable membrane between inside and out is typical of these island houses. I love the old jalousie windows that tilt to let in the breeze but keep out the rain, which in Hawaii comes at least once a day during certain seasons. The fixtures follow the same template as the kitchen, with a similar terrazzo countertop. And we did the same kind of concrete floor with integral color. The material absorbs the color in an uneven way, so there's a lot of dimension and swirl to it. The final result has an aqueous quality.

And that takes us back to the island and this magical place that seems to exist in a slower, less stressful world. It's time out of time. It's paradise.

ABOVE: If it's too rainy or cold to go outdoors, you can always shower inside. The shower stall has a mermaid etched on the glass door. (I wish you could see her!) The concrete floor is durable and can handle any sand and dirt that's tracked in from outside, yet it still has a luminous, watery appearance. I used a large mirror over the vanity to expand the space, but it's still framed by the woodwork instead of going from wall to wall—that would be too contemporary. OPPOSITE: When I bought the table, its seats were already covered in that vintage tropical print. The Chinese chair is a nod to the Asian influences you see all through these old Hawaiian houses.

MALIBU, CALIFORNIA

Remember Gull Cottage? It was the charming house on the English seacoast where Gene Tierney goes to live in *The Ghost and Mrs. Muir*. This New England Revival house, one of the oldest in Malibu, had some of that same quality. I can just see Tierney falling asleep by the fire while her dashing sea captain, Rex Harrison, tucks a blanket around her and looks on fondly.

The house had so many pretty touches, like the Tudor detailing, the second-floor balconies overlooking the ocean, and the tiny panes of glass in the exterior doors. The challenge for architect Oscar Shamamian and me was to redo the interiors while still making them look as if they had always been exactly this way.

The client wanted a big country kitchen, open and airy. She likes to cook and the kitchen is the hub of a Chekhovian house party of family and friends on weekends and holidays. Oscar designed simple cabinets with traditional hardware. Countertops are made of butcher block, which feels homey and humble. But behind the old-fashioned cupboard doors are modern conveniences like dishwashers and refrigerator drawers. The island is big and roomy and offers a mix of cupboards and open shelves. It's packed with practical storage for everything from cookbooks to large trays. The cooktop is centered on top because this client is a very social cook. She wants to be right in the middle of things while she works. We added a custom hood with a bronze finish, which won't get pitted in the salt air. And then we wrapped it with a pot rack, so she can see all her pots and pans at once and reach up and get what she wants. It's festooned with baskets as well, which makes a big, bulky hood look almost whimsical.

The terrace is right on the ocean, with an old, gnarled angel's trumpet tree arching over the dining table. FOLLOWING SPREAD: We took down walls and opened the kitchen to the rest of the house. There's a fireplace nearby, with a dining table in front of it. The table has a built-in lazy Susan—very convenient for passing things around, family-style.

The master bathroom was carved out of a series of smaller rooms to make this light and airy space, with white walls and an old-fashioned floor made up of tiny tiles by Ann Sacks. The breeze runs right through the room when you open the French doors opposite the tub, and walk out onto a balcony facing the ocean.

The tub is in its own niche but it's not small and tight. Nothing in here feels cramped. A mirror framed in wood and divided into three parts, which makes it look more vintage, reflects the sunlight and the view. I like the twin vanities, with a dressing table in the center, which run along one wall. They're very ladylike and I can imagine Gene Tierney sitting on that Chinese Chippendale chair and brushing out her hair. But then the dark wooden tables are a little unexpected. They look more like relics from one of the sea captain's voyages. The nineteenth-century Japanese table in the center has a fascinating shape, curved where its equally interesting neighbor is angular. Together, they tip what could have been a very feminine room back toward the masculine, and that gives it a much more interesting ambiguity.

The oriel window is an elegant touch between the two silvery mirrors. That's one of my favorite Bennison fabrics on the slipper chair. I love those luscious grapes and there's something about that tea-dyed linen—it has such a beautiful hand, as the fabric manufacturers say.

TOWN

BEL AIR, CALIFORNIA

Just think of this as my Edwin Lutyens moment. Lutyens was the great British architect who designed all those charming yet strong-boned English country houses around the turn of the century, and I like to think he, too, would have done something like this if he had been confronted with a 1950s ranch house in Los Angeles.

Basically, I tore it down and rebuilt it, with old brick and old stone and old wood. I always knew the house had problems, but I bought it anyway, because it was on a lush, secluded piece of property shaded by towering eucalyptus trees. I just didn't realize at the time that I would wind up completely redoing it. Oscar Shamamian and I reconfigured the floor plan and changed the proportions of the rooms. I was constrained by the original footprint of the house—I couldn't build beyond it—and the kitchen is smaller than I would have liked. But there are ways to design around that so you hardly notice.

It starts with the floor plan. The laundry, the pantry, and the kitchen are laid out as a sequence of rooms, culminating in a breakfast room in the shape of an octagon. The big, wide doorways between each room line up, so you can stand in one and look all the way through to the others. It's a classic technique, called an enfilade, that you see in many grand European houses. And it lets you borrow space, in a way. The architecture sets up the vista, and the eye automatically goes to the farthest point. So the kitchen feels much larger than it actually is.

The barrel-vaulted ceiling also helps. Lutyens was a connoisseur of shape, and he loved a barrel vault. It gives a sense of ceremony to a narrow space. You really feel as if this could be part of some wonderful old English country house. I wanted to play up the idea that this was a great old service kitchen—admittedly, a much smaller version of something you might see in one of those movies like *Gosford Park* or *The Remains of the Day*, where the house is so visually compelling that it practically becomes another character.

This kitchen is grand and modest at the same time, with that vaulted ceiling and cabinetry that's straight out of the servant's quarters. The cupboards are plain and white, but there's something unusual about the hardware. Every piece, including the faucets and the doorknobs, is plated with sterling so it has the subtle gleam of old silver. It's a look that you just can't get any other way, softer and more beautiful than nickel. And it's a finish that moves and changes, shifting with the light.

I like the fact that it's not static. Same thing with the Lagos Azul limestone countertops. Citrus stains them. Every once in a while, I'll have them professionally cleaned and polished and resealed, but you have to accept the fact that they will get marred. It's funny; people admire old stone, but when it comes to their own house, they want something pristine. Not me. I see the beauty in imperfection.

The octagonal breakfast room is like a little temple in the garden, with five pairs of French doors that lead to a terrace paved in Turkish travertine. I leave them open all the time, so my dogs can run in and out. Eating in this room is the closest thing to eating outdoors. You're sheltered from the sun, but you still have the sensation of being out in the garden.

The breakfast room, at the end of an enfilade of rooms that spans the laundry, the pantry, and the kitchen, is like the light at the end of a tunnel.

Sometimes I think the character of a whole house is embodied in the floors. Here, they're made of old fumed oak, and they're just waxed. No urethane. Everybody tried to talk me out of it, but putting anything else but wax on them just doesn't give you the same effect. This way, they have the patina of fine antique furniture. I try to walk the walk. If I have counters that are not impervious to stains and floors that need to be waxed, then I can say with great confidence to my clients, hey, don't be afraid. It requires some maintenance, but it's worth it.

The wood floor brings such warmth to a breakfast room that is practically all windows. It's shaped like an octagon, and I hope Lutyens would approve. It may be unfashionable these days to define rooms instead of leaving it all one giant merged space, but I think most people actually like pleasing geometries and regular shapes.

It's a handsome room, what I would call masculine English rather than pretty English. There's no chintz. The curtains are made from hemp, in the Moghul Panel pattern from my Jasper collection. It's modeled on a vintage Indian textile that I became obsessed with and had remade. When they're all drawn shut, the room feels like a tent.

The ceiling rises to a peak and is painted in lime wash, which is not a perfectly solid paint. You can see the brushstrokes and the variations in color they left behind. It dries unevenly to a chalky finish that catches the light in different ways. I love that kind of thing, which you get with natural materials. It gives you the touch of the hand.

ABOVE: This is actually a galley kitchen—not the most promising situation—but you never even notice because your eye is drawn to the ceiling with its beautiful barrel vault. The glass-fronted refrigerator and cupboards also help by giving you a sense that there's more depth. OPPOSITE: George III mahogany chairs surround a William IV pedestal table made of rosewood. The floor is made of reclaimed fumed oak from Baba, a place in North Carolina that sells really beautiful antique floors. Here, the boards are laid in an octagonal pattern. The painted wood-and-metal lantern is from my Jasper collection.

I did some research before I bought a stove and decided that a BlueStar was the best professional stove you can get for a house. Frankly, I think I fell in love with it because I really wanted that raised griddle and the infrared broiler. Don't get me wrong—I don't actually cook. I just liked the look of it, and it's actually very useful for grilled cheese sandwiches.

Oscar designed the hood—very Jules Verne meets the Industrial Revolution—with metal straps and screws, all in an antique pewter finish. It makes the stove look even more massive than it is and turns it into a dramatic focal point.

Everything else in here seems plain by comparison, but I'm always impressed with how functional the whole layout is. A galley kitchen turns out to be exceptionally efficient.

ABOVE LEFT: In the bar area, I installed a convenient under-the-counter wine refrigerator. On the backsplash, handmade Moroccan Bejmat tiles from Ann Sacks are all slightly different shades of white. I like them for their opalescent quality. The grout is tinted taupe to suggest age. ABOVE RIGHT: The 60-inch BlueStar RNB Heritage Classic range has six burners and two extra-large ovens, in addition to my coveted broiler. OPPOSITE: Both the pantry sink and the faucet are from my Country collection for Kallista. The Lagos Azul limestone on the countertop is from Walker Zanger. PREVIOUS SPREAD: Here, you can see the enfilade from kitchen to pantry to laundry. The sink and faucet on the right are from my Town collection for Kallista. I found the hanging lights at Ann-Morris Antiques.

This is a room that fuses the idea of closet and bath and still manages to look open and luxurious and elegant.

The master bath was a challenge because the square footage I had to work with was limited. I could either have a big bathroom or a big walk-in closet. I could not have both—until I decided to combine them.

The solution was so simple. I put the bathtub in the center of the room and lined the perimeter with built-in closets. Since the bathtub was going to be so prominent, it was really important to me to get the shape right. I wanted something that felt like Claridge's hotel in the 1930s—rounded forms, very sculptural, and above all, big. I love to take baths, and I like to stretch out and be comfortable. When I was doing this house, there was very little plumbing related to this period, so I had to design it all myself, and it became my Town tub and faucet for Kallista.

It's very dramatic to have a tub in the center of the room, but where are you going to put all those things you need within arm's reach, like bath oil and a cell phone and towels? I solved that problem with a rolling cart, an antique piece made of ebonized wood that looked very elegant and was super practical.

It's a room devoted to dressing and undressing. The wall-to-wall closets have French doors, with the upper panels made of glass so you can see exactly what's inside them. On one wall, the closets pause to make room for a built-in vanity and a large mirror. The vanity is fitted with lots of drawers, which looks more old-fashioned and reminds me of a piece of furniture. The fourth wall of the room is made up of French doors that open to the terrace.

ABOVE: I turned a hallway connecting a guest room and bath into a dressing area, with two closets separated by a chest of drawers. OPPOSITE: In the master bath, the built-in vanity is equipped with two sinks and a lot of storage space. The mirror above it goes all the way up to the ceiling, but it's beveled and done in sections, so it feels more 1930s. A Savonarola stool provides a place to sit while you're getting in or out of your clothes. I installed radiant heat under the Italian limestone floor, so your feet would never be cold in the morning. A vintage Chinese rug brings in more color and warmth.

Onyx is cheaper than a Jackson Pollock and it can have a similar effect, especially when the pattern is as wild and otherworldly as this. It's Egyptian onyx, so I immediately had all these images in my head of the old Shepheard's Hotel in Cairo and Agatha Christie's *Death on the Nile*. I thought that lining the shower room with this amazing stone would add a kind of British Colonial aura. It was a big, extravagant gesture, which I love. But when I first put it up, I panicked. Was it too much?

This is why designers don't want their clients to see a room until it's all done. As soon as all the various fixtures and accessories were in, the onyx looked fine. It seemed to bathe the room in color and warmth. You felt as if you had stepped inside a Fabergé egg or some extraordinary jewel box. It took the idea of a 1930s hotel bathroom up another level.

There's really nothing else you can do in a bathroom that has quite the impact of a fabulous piece of stone. It's instant drama and it connotes luxury, elevating the whole experience.

ABOVE LEFT: The shower door is made of glass, so you can see straight through to the showpiece of the room—the Sunset onyx. I wanted fixtures with a 1930s look and designed these as part of my Town collection for Kallista. ABOVE RIGHT: The onyx slabs are accented with horizontal bands, to suggest an old-fashioned wainscot and create a play of pattern on pattern. A vintage nickel cart holds towels. OPPOSITE: The clear glass on the closet doors changes to handmade mirrored glass above. It has a cloudy, ethereal look that is echoed in the alabaster dish light that hangs from the center of the cove ceiling. PREVIOUS SPREAD: Had he thought of it, Louis XIV would have loved a tub like this, open to the garden. The fixtures are from my Town collection for Kallista.

HOLLYWOOD HILLS, CALIFORNIA

It's good to be reminded that size isn't everything. In fact, if you ask a professional chef they will probably tell you that a small kitchen is much more efficient than a large kitchen. And it can also be elegant as well, as we proved in this little gem of a house, built in 1947 in the Hollywood Hills.

Here, you have the classic kitchen triangle of sink, stove, and refrigerator (unseen, but it's opposite the sink). Every inch of cabinetry is fitted out as skillfully as in a boat. For example, the corner cabinet to the left of the sink opens up and then rotates out, so you can see everything inside it at a glance and reach for the pot you need. The little table by the door was built at counter height, so it can double as an extra workspace. Or you can sit on a stool and have a cup of coffee and an English muffin on the run.

One thing we did was to make the Carrara marble countertops extra-thick. Normally they're three quarters of an inch. These are an inch and a half. You can actually buy a thicker marble slab, or you can cheat it by chamfering the edge and adding a thicker strip of marble. Either way, it makes the countertop feel more solid and substantial and, as a result, the whole room feels more elegant.

An early English gaslight, now electrified, hangs over the breakfast table and adds an antique note. It makes the kitchen feel special. The palette is all creams and taupes. Open shelves display a collection of hotel silver.

In a small powder room, I kept the palette deliberately monochromatic to create a sense of calm. But I chose interesting textures—old wood, smooth marble, and squares of tea paper on the walls—to catch the eye and add layers of depth.

This is a small, charming house, with only two bedrooms. But that doesn't mean you have to think of it as small. Instead, I treated each room as a little jewel box, and hung wallpaper where I wanted to add richness and draped silk to make a romantic canopy over the master bed.

This powder room also happens to double as a guest bath, thanks to a small shower. But that meant there wasn't room for much else. The cabinet that holds the sink is a copy of an early nineteenth-century Swedish commode. Its demilune shape is pretty, but in this case it's also practical. It takes up less space, which makes it easier to walk around it. By eliminating those sharp right angles, you don't have to worry about people bumping into it.

I love Swedish furniture because it has these iconic shapes, but done in a way that's more informal than the French equivalent. You rarely see gilding. The wood is usually painted or scrubbed. It's less fancy, which makes it more approachable and better suited to a house like this that has no pretensions to grandeur.

But I still wanted even this powder room to be beautiful. So I lined the walls with squares of tea paper from Gracie, the venerable wallpaper company that was founded in New York City in 1898 and is still run by the same family. This handmade paper is not shiny, as people usually think of tea paper. In fact, it's very matte and since it's cut into squares, it looks almost like blocks of limestone. It makes a small room feel instantly elegant.

There's a weathered softness to the carved honey-colored wood on the Swedish-style commode. I paired an oval sink made of hammered metal with my Town faucet in nickel silver. The swing-arm sconce, from my collection for Jasper, is a reproduction of a French original. Delicate matchstick blinds filter the sun that pours in from the garden outside.

LOS ANGELES, CALIFORNIA

A family that cooks together stays together, and this is the kind of kitchen where everyone can gather round. It's big and inviting, with plenty of places to sit. The kids treat it like a clubhouse and are constantly in and out with their friends. The idea is functional, but not fancy. There are no elaborately carved Louis XIV-style legs on the island, and it's not topped with some knockout stone, just sturdy, no-nonsense butcher block. This is a work surface. These people really like to cook, and you could feed an army from that huge Wolf range. The tiles behind it are not decorated with cute little pictures of fruit or squirrels. They're simple and handmade, in an earthy shade of bisque.

And even though the kitchen is large, the actual cooking triangle is compact, with stove, sink, and refrigerator within a few steps of each other. One person can make dinner without running a marathon. It's an old-fashioned kitchen that functions in a modern way. There's a traditional butler's pantry, but also a desk with a computer—command central—for Mom. French doors open to a large dining terrace with a fireplace, so you can eat indoors or out. Everything has a relaxed quality, just like those stools at the island, chosen for comfort without any concern for whether they actually matched anything else. And the cabinets are painted my favorite pale green—a color that has a little age in it—instead of the ubiquitous white.

The hanging lights look as if they could have come out of a 1930s candy shop. I found the old glass shades at a flea market. To the left of the stove, there's a door to the dining room that swings in and out and has a little window in it—another old-fashioned touch.

This house is a hybrid—a fusion of a traditional English manor with a warm, expansive Mediterranean villa that opens to the outdoors. It's relaxed and luxurious but not overdone.

The his-and-hers dressing rooms combine romance and practicality. His is more straightforward, efficiently fitted out to take advantage of the galley layout. Then the balcony adds a grace note and makes it feel larger. Hers is prettier, with neoclassical mirrored doors that convey elegance and make the room seem lighter, brighter, and bigger.

The master bathroom picks up on the openness, with casement windows that overlook the treetops. And it builds on the romance with a large mirror over the tub—made with antiqued glass, because there's a limit to how much reality any human body can actually bear. But what really makes the room feel luxurious is the sofa. The addition of that one piece of furniture transforms its character. A bathroom transcends its basic practicality to become a place where you'd want to sit and relax. The sofa meant that the couple could stop and be together while they were dressing to go out. That time became more special to them, personal and intimate and very welcome since they have a life that normally revolves around their children. But this bathroom is just for the two of them.

ABOVE: In his dressing room, a leather-topped bench provides a place to sit. The balcony staircase leads down to a Jacuzzi. OPPOSITE: Her bench is more curvaceous and topped with linen velvet. The X motif on the doors is repeated on the hanging lamp. FOLLOWING SPREAD: The matching mirrors over the vanity are made of clear glass, unlike the more romantic version over the tub. The faucets, sinks, and tub are from my Town collection for Kallista.

BRENTWOOD, CALIFORNIA

Remember Cary Grant and Katharine Hepburn chasing a leopard through that great old Connecticut house in *Bringing Up Baby*? Well, this California house has some of that same wonderful feeling, just on a larger scale. It was designed by the renowned architect Paul R. Williams for ZaSu Pitts and built in 1936. I'm very respectful of these finely detailed, very personal Hollywood houses, but they were done in an era when there was a sharp distinction between public and private spaces. Now people want to erase that divide and invite everyone into the kitchen, so architect Brian Tichenor got rid of all the boxy servant spaces and opened the whole thing up.

But we did it in a way that stayed true to the 1930s narrative of the house. The new countertops are made of traditional poured terrazzo, with an old-fashioned metal edge. The metal is attractive and also super-practical: it protects the edge so things can't bang into it and chip the counter. Many of these old kitchens had vinyl or cork tiles on the floors—again, practical because they're easy on the feet, and if you drop a glass often it won't break. I decided to go with vinyl tile, but not the classic black and white. I thought it might look too aggressive, so we chose green and white. It was more unexpected, yet still dark enough to create contrast and neutral enough to recede into the backdrop.

This is a kitchen for people who really cook, and you can see that by such details as the knives hanging on the wall within easy reach and the spices right above the stove. There's no attempt to hide the pots, which sit on an open shelf under the island, or the utensils, which are not relegated to a drawer. Instead they're ready and waiting, gathered into an old milk pail, right in the center of things. All the tools that are essential to cooking become part of the décor.

This is a family kitchen, and there's something so inviting about having a real table where the kids can sit and play or do homework while Mom and Dad cook. The French bistro chairs are more comfortable than the usual stools alongside an island. The kitchen, framed by a graceful arch, is the hub of the house, and it flows naturally into the family room.

Sometimes you just want glamour—sheer, unabashed,
Ginger Rogers and Fred Astaire–style glamour.

That's what we were aiming for here. The oval tub is encased in what looks almost like a sarcophagus of marble, curved to match its contours. On the Venetian plaster wall, hung low enough so you can see yourself in it while bathing, is a beautiful Venetian glass mirror. And then I found that little mirrored table, which looks straight out of a 1930s movie, the kind where the heroine doesn't have a mere bedroom. She has a boudoir.

All those mirrored surfaces reflect light, and then you have the added glint from the antique silver sconces and the polished nickel fixtures. The room has a sense of sparkle. It wraps you up in the romantic notion of lying back and luxuriating in this long, lovely tub, lit only by candlelight. You feel as if you've been transported to another era, when a bath was a sybaritic pleasure, the body soothed with unguents and oils.

And there's something undeniably sexy about taking a bath in public, if you know what I mean. This tub is not tucked away in some little room. It feels as if it's out in the open, with that staircase in the background. You've suddenly become the star of your own movie, like one of those fetching actresses who splashed around in bubble baths on-screen.

The basic layouts of the bedroom and bath were already present, but the closets were inadequate. So, we had an idea: we found enough space on the third floor to make a dressing room, and then we constructed that staircase to get to it. By opening it up instead of closing it off behind the wall, it became a feature of the room. The iron stair rail with those delicate, wedding-cake loops is modeled on one that we saw in another Paul R. Williams house. We just borrowed his vocabulary and recreated it here.

SANTA MONICA, CALIFORNIA

This is the most photogenic house I've ever seen, and that's probably because it was designed by a man who knew exactly what would look good on camera—Cedric Gibbons. He was a great Hollywood art director, responsible for the look of everything from *The Wizard of Oz* to *The Philadelphia Story*. And in his extravagant sets for the Busby Berkeley musicals, he basically created art deco on-screen and then other designers followed.

Someone had already redone the kitchen when my client bought the house, which was built in 1930, and I thought the Bulthaup cabinets were a good choice. Their strong, lean lines seemed to go with the pure, aerodynamic lines of the house's Streamline Moderne vocabulary. And I liked how the room was split, with white cabinetry around the perimeter and a stainless steel island in the middle, so you got a two-tone effect, kind of like a black-and-white movie. But the kitchen needed more of a story line if it was going to live up to the rest of the house.

Sometimes a gesture will do it. If you add just a few elements that evoke the period, your eye and your imagination will convince you that the rest of the room is equally true to form. So I brought in those great leather-and-chrome bar stools with sleek tubular legs, like something Warren McArthur could have designed. I found the perfect art deco light fixtures to hang over the island. And then I gave the kitchen a focal point with that graphic art deco clock.

If you think the kitchen is great, just wait till you see the bathroom that Gibbons designed for his wife, the silent-film star Dolores del Rio. She was an exotic creature, and famously alluring. Orson Welles once called her "the most beautiful woman I have ever seen," and Gibbons was clearly devoted to her. Everything in her room was conceived to enhance and enshrine her beauty. A dressing table is built into one wall, which is mirrored from end to end. But the mirror stops before it gets to the ceiling to make room for a clerestory window that floods the space with natural light. You want all the natural light you can get if you're putting on makeup. The dressing table itself is made of floating planes of glass balanced on blond wood drawers that are stepped, like a staircase, and hold makeup and toiletries. The whole thing was a vision, and luckily it had been perfectly maintained. The only thing I had to do was insinuate a shower into the room, without tampering with it.

The house resembles an ocean liner, ready to set sail. The style is very geometric and pure. The original designers established a vocabulary and then used it for every detail. I like the way the pavers on the lawn mimic the shape of the windowpanes. The whole property was conceived as a unified composition. FOLLOWING SPREAD: I love that floating plane above the island. It gives you that sense of motion embodied in all the zooming horizontal lines of Streamline Moderne architecture. The black rubber floor runs throughout the house and looks like something you'd see in a German submarine. Gibbons initially used it to create a seamless backdrop for all the dancing girls in the Busby Berkeley musicals. The bar stools are by York Street Studio.

I had a different challenge in a building we built from scratch to house a gym. What should the bathroom look like? The space was small, and most people would probably have made it white, thinking that would make it seem larger. But I went with black instead, because something interesting happens in a small room when you use a dark color. The dark walls seem to dissolve, and you lose all sense of boundaries. But I didn't use black paint. I chose black granite—honed, not polished. I decided there would be enough shine from the mirror, and besides, I wanted a surface that drew you in, rather than hit you in the face. And honed granite just feels softer. Then I balanced the black with a white pedestal sink for contrast. The art deco sconces tell you what period we're in. The room picks up on the vocabulary of the house and once again, it makes you feel as if you've stepped into one of Gibbons's beautifully designed black-and-white movies.

ABOVE LEFT: That stepped-ceiling detail is a motif used throughout the house, so I borrowed it for the bathroom in the new gym building. The porthole on the door also fits in with all the 1930s imagery. The sink, fixtures, and mirror are part of my Loft line for Kallista. ABOVE RIGHT: The main powder room in the house has walls covered in silver leaf that looks like molten metal. The table is another exercise in floating planes. OPPOSITE: In Dolores del Rio's bathroom the dressing table takes up one whole wall, but since it's primarily made of glass and mirrors, it feels very ethereal. I think any woman would feel beautiful putting on her makeup here.

BEVERLY HILLS, CALIFORNIA

I magine showering under a waterfall. That's how it feels to step into this room, which is more glass than wall. You don't feel as if you're enclosed. You feel like you're out in the garden.

This was the first bathroom I ever built for myself, and I wanted to stay within the vocabulary of the 1960s house—modern, spare, and minimal, with a certain handmade quality. Since I needed a steam shower, I decided to extend the space with a glass cube. Actually, two of the walls are faced in a limestone that doesn't even register as a color and almost disappears, like wet sand.

In doing this room, I learned that it's possible to create a tremendous amount of romance with the simplest of materials—stone, wood, water, and light. You don't need a lot of decoration to tell a story. Sometimes I would be soaking in that tub alongside those azure glass tiles and feel as if I were in the Aegean . . . or inside a Japanese shogun's palace, with all those strong vertical and horizontal planes of wood. It was constantly morphing into different places and periods in my imagination. This project was done way before I designed my own line of bath fixtures, and I had to cobble together the shower and faucets out of various industrial parts, the kinds of things that, at the time, you only saw in hospitals.

It's interesting—when you go into a bathroom, you're stripped of your armor, in a sense, and psychologically you need to feel protected. Some bathrooms can be too open, too exposed. I was concerned that all that glass might make me uncomfortable, but what saved it was the fact that the garden just beyond was surrounded by a wall and completely private. I also had it lit with outdoor lights so it wouldn't turn into a black hole at night and take on an ominous aspect. Even at midnight, it looks inviting.

ABOVE: This is all about stripping down to the bare essentials and coming clean. Even the ceiling is glass, which makes it kind of crazy to take a shower while it's raining. One limestone wall forms an integral bench, so you can sit down in the steam and just stop and clear your head. OPPOSITE: The Venetian plaster wall and the glass tiles around Kohler's whirlpool tub have texture and depth. They're not perfectly straight and smooth. You can feel the touch of the hand that troweled the wall and shaped the tiles. I added the little pear wood and leather Hermès stool, where you can toss your clothes or just sit down for a moment to put on your shoes.

With all that exposed wood, the house has an elemental quality. It makes me think of Asia, especially after I added simple matchstick blinds and vintage Chinese chairs.

I did something here I don't normally do; I put the stove in the center of the kitchen. My friend Cindy Crawford had recently rented a house in the Hamptons that had a similar configuration, and I noticed that it was convivial and so much fun. Everyone just gravitated to the kitchen, and she could cook and talk to her guests instead of facing a wall.

One small problem: there was a post right in the middle of my kitchen. The architect Michael Kovac and I had taken down a wall that originally divided the space into a small galley kitchen and a maid's room, but we couldn't get rid of that supporting post. So, how do you turn a disadvantage into an advantage? I decided to sandblast it to bring out the grain of the wood, and I used it to anchor the island. Then I put a cherry top on the island and painted the rest of it cream, so you had the impression of this floating horizontal plane juxtaposed to the vertical post. Recessed squares for wine bottles on one side echoed the simple geometries.

Instead of letting the stainless steel appliances fall where they may, I ganged them up and put them all against one wall. It has more impact and also looks more organized that way. And it turned out to be a very practical layout, with the classic kitchen triangle completed by a sink under the window, where you can rinse the dishes and look out at the canyon. There's a lot of scrub and brush and eucalyptus outside, and I wanted that same gray-green color on the kitchen cabinets. With all the wood and the gray-green and the plaster on the walls tinted with a little burnt sienna, the kitchen felt like a natural extension of the landscape.

ABOVE: I found a Jean Prouvé table at an antiques show in New York and surrounded it with mismatched Chinese chairs. I've always loved the look of those chairs—strong, severe, like a sculpture made out of wood. This became the breakfast area.
OPPOSITE: It's the old campfire idea—everything happens around the cooktop on the center island. The hood needed to be a little higher so it did not interrupt the sight lines, which meant I had to have one custom-made one with an extra-strong ventilation system. I thought that the cherry top on the island might be difficult to maintain, but it wasn't. I just kept it oiled and it was fine. The rest of the counters are a limestone that looks like concrete and blends right in with the muted palette.

The dining room looks into the entry courtyard, where I whitewashed the wall to give it that Greek-island quality. It makes a nice contrast with the wood and the stones and the terra-cotta tiles. The Spanish refectory table and the dining chairs are equally simple and plain.

UPPER EAST SIDE, MANHATTAN

I'm not sure if Nick and Nora Charles, the witty husband-and-wife detective team from *The Thin Man* movies, ever went into their kitchen—except to get ice for their martinis—but I imagine it might have looked something like this. This is my version of that type of 1930s staff kitchen—clean, white, and practical—with a touch of green. I use green so often that I think of it as a neutral. It's also one of the few colors that always looks clean to me.

When I first walked into this room, it had pine cabinets and a heart carved into the hood, very "country with a K." We painted the cabinetry and resurfaced everything to make it feel more urbane. The perimeter counters are done in a blue-green limestone that picks up the shade of the celadon green tiles on the backsplash. Then the island is pure white, for contrast. It's constructed with a big thick slab of CaesarStone on top that won't stain or scratch, no matter how much use it gets. And since the couple who live here like to entertain, it gets used a lot. It works as a prep area and a service table, offering a large flat surface where the caterers can plate the food.

I tried something a little bit different on the floor. It's made of a self-leveling industrial cement-like material called Ardex. We didn't really have the depth to do terrazzo, so this seemed like a good substitute. Plus, you can get the most interesting colors, like this beautiful khaki.

To me, this kitchen has one foot in the romantic past and the other in the super-efficient present. You can see that most clearly in the Viking range, where we had the oven doors enameled in white to feel more old-fashioned and take you back to Manhattan in the 1930s. But the nice thing about doing this kind of kitchen today is that you don't have to give up a single bit of modern technology. You can still have a blender that really blends and a toaster that makes flawless toast, because there are plenty of new models with a retro look. In fact, they're so good looking that we decided to leave them out on the counter. They're part of the charm.

I like the way the touches of green in this kitchen make the white look even more white and crisp and clean. The sturdy oak stools were copied from a late nineteenth-century original and are actually very comfortable, with a metal rail around the bottom to rest your feet on. The centerpiece of the room is a pot rack hung with gleaming copper pots. They're incredibly decorative—like a piece of good jewelry—and they also happen to be great from a technical standpoint as well. Copper conducts heat better than any other metal, and many professional chefs will use nothing else.

If you look at old photographs of the dining room on the Queen Mary, you'll see furniture that resembles this. There's something very White Star Line about this breakfast room.

I love the light here. It overlooks the East River and it gets that pure, clean, crystalline light of early morning, which is why it's such a pleasure to have breakfast in this room.

The amazing art deco lantern is the piece your eye immediately goes to, and it sets the tone. The silver casing is handsome and feels very substantial. Then there's the surprise of the deep blue glass, so bold and unexpected, bringing a vibrant note of color into the room. The walls seem to pick it up and reflect it in their paler blue.

The chairs are English art deco, made in the 1930s. I've noticed something interesting about English art deco: it often doesn't have the extraordinary whimsy and flights of imagination that you find in its French counterparts. There's something a little more stolid about it, and you can see it in these chairs. They really haven't quite let go of traditional forms. They're beautifully carved, but they're still familiar and very comforting. They remind me of something you might see on a British ocean liner or in a 1930s tearoom.

I was originally told the table was English, but it turns out to be Continental. It's a pretty piece, with that sculptural base tiered like a wedding cake. The dark mahogany furniture is a nice contrast to the lightness of the rest of the room. It keeps it all from floating away in the river light.

ABOVE: Old family pieces mix with modern acquisitions in the table settings. I love the hand-painted Imari plates. OPPOSITE: The breakfast room feels airy, even with the dark furniture. I hung a Venetian mirror on the wall to reflect the river and the light. Photographs from the client's collection seemed to have the kind of stillness I wanted. An old-fashioned swinging door leads into the kitchen.

I think of this as the perfect Manhattan bathroom. That huge window looks out over the East River, and you could lie back in the Jacuzzi tub and see the twinkling lights of the city reflected in the mirror. The design is very simple—no gilt, no ostentation, no fuss—yet every detail is exquisitely crafted. Look at the beautifully molded edge on the marble. And the marble itself is unusual, because of the color—a very pale Ming green. We used it to surround the tub and top the vanity and cover the floor. All that marble sets the tone. The room looks seamless, which creates a feeling of serenity.

White towels are stacked on shelves, conveniently within reach of anyone stepping out of the tub. Cream silk curtains just brush the floor. A vintage French chair by Jacques Adnet is nearby, if you want to sit down for a moment, or just toss your robe on it. Instead of mirroring the whole wall alongside the tub, I chose to do discrete panels of mirror. That feels somehow more French to me, and more 1930s. Also, when you divide it like that, the mirror starts to suggest the panes of a window. And it fractures the reflection of the room in a more interesting way.

ABOVE: The mirrored medicine chest, part of my Town line for Kallista, is framed in mirror as well, just like the panels over the tub. The Town sconces are fitted with a faceted Baccarat crystal lens in front—a technique used in antique pieces to augment the candlelight. OPPOSITE: The natural light is crystalline in this room, and I wanted nothing dark to interrupt it. Everything is creamy white or pale green. The Town fixtures on the tub add a glint of silver that is echoed in the panels of the mirror. Anything vertical, like those panels, is going to increase the sense of height. The overhead light fixture is by another French master craftsman, René Lalique.

I can just see Carole Lombard, in a white silk-charmeuse sheath, flirting with her dinner partner at the mirrored table in this penthouse suite. When the owners of the Lowell hotel asked me to redo it, I was happy to oblige. The Lowell was my home away from home in New York. I knew exactly how it should look—elegant, sophisticated, with all the glamour I remembered from those gorgeous 1930s movies.

The suite, with three bedrooms, is on the same scale as an apartment. You could live here quite happily, and it's a fabulous place for entertaining, with three terraces and spectacular views of the city. The best place for the dining table was under the greenhouse glass, where mahogany would look out of place. Wouldn't it be more interesting if the table were made of mirror and reflected all that sunlight? Then it would practically dematerialize. And imagine how it would look in candlelight—like a bottomless pool. It's the kind of table where you are virtually obligated to drink champagne and, with any luck, the conversation will be equally scintillating.

The floor is paved in honed marble to make it feel more like a French conservatory, and for that of course you need a few palms. Then I redid the built-in armoire on the side to hold glassware, china, table linens, and silver—all conveniently within reach. The kitchen was compact, to say the least—a mere 70 square feet. But it's a model of efficiency, with a 24-inch electric cooktop and an 18-inch dishwasher by Miele and a 27-inch Sub-Zero refrigerator. Everything else you need is hidden behind those brushed aluminum doors on the Poggenpohl cabinetry. It's beautifully designed and so elegantly simple that it creates this feeling of serenity. You feel compelled to be organized and keep the space uncluttered in order to live up to it. A CaesarStone countertop in concrete continues the soft gray palette. It also eliminates one potential problem: you don't have to worry about stains because it's impervious to them—even lemon juice—and if you rest a hot pot on it, it won't leave a ring. It's an amazingly functional, anxiety-free kitchen.

ABOVE: There's a refrigerator on the left, hiding behind Poggenpohl's AL series aluminum panels, and an oven tucked under the Miele cooktop. I designed the Loft faucet with lever handles for Kallista and paired it with an extra-deep stainless steel sink by Franke. OPPOSITE: The dining table from Jean de Merry reminds me of one of French designer Serge Roche's fanciful mirrored tables from the 1930s. I had the Louis XVI–style chairs covered in soft leather the color of elephant skin. The honed marble tiles in Light Smoke on the floor are from Ann Sacks.

I wanted to take you back to another era, when men wore dinner jackets and women clasped on diamond bracelets before they went out for the evening.

This dressing room and bath could have stepped right off the silver screen. It's a very 1930s look, with the hanging alabaster light and the marble vanity balanced on slim, walking-stick legs made of fluted nickel. The walls, counters, and floors are covered in creamy Selene marble with celadon green and gold veins. It's like the most luxurious form of wallpaper, enveloping the space and making it feel very rich.

The dressing table is mirrored, and set in front of it is a Klismos-style chair upholstered in cognac-colored leather. The mirror on the wall is framed in wavy plaster like icing on a cake—another Serge Roche–inspired touch. The opaline glass sconces on either side feel very Busby Berkeley, Radio City Music Hall. They form a colonnade of light that's repeated again and again in the reflections of the mirrors. Because the dressing table and the vanity are placed opposite each other, the mirrors reflect each other and create this perpetual recession of space. It's infinity in an intimate room, and it makes the bath feel larger.

Whenever you expose the plumbing under a sink, as we did here, the hardware above and below has to be beautifully finished. I like the open look. It contributes to the old-fashioned feeling. This was an era that predates the more suburban built-in vanity. What you don't see in these photographs is a deep soaking tub on the left, with a window looking out on the city. There's also a shower on the right and two individual wood-paneled dressing rooms near the dressing table. It's a perfectly appointed suite in a full-service hotel. All you have to do is walk in, and immediately you feel pampered.

OPPOSITE: The Town faucets from my line for Kallista and the vanity legs set the muted silvery tone. They're finished in polished nickel. The Horton alabaster bowl light from Vaughan is also trimmed in the same soft nickel, and so are the Berling sconces from Ralph Lauren Home. The Selene honed marble on the walls and floor is from Ann Sacks. On the floor, it's bordered in polished Costa Esmeralda granite from Artistic Tile, which gives it that extra level of detail. ABOVE: There's a mirror-upon-mirror effect in the dressing room. A vanity mirror from John Rosselli stands on Nancy Corzine's Versailles mirrored desk and is great for putting on makeup. The Serge mirror on the wall is from Dessin Fournir. I love the lines of that Klismos-style chair—with its curved back and legs—from John Rosselli.

EATON SQUARE, LONDON

In one of those classic London town houses (actually, this apartment encompassed three), filled with fine antiques and glorious art and exotic fabrics, this kitchen felt almost like a palate cleanser. When I first saw the space, it was already outfitted with Bulthaup cabinetry, which is as minimal and modern as you can get. It was cool and white and self-effacing, a very well-designed and beautifully made built-in kitchen. Why fix what isn't broken? I decided to leave it there.

The countertops and backsplash wall were done in a pale, almost Nordic-looking gray granite, which offered a nice contrast to all the white. The effect was quiet and tonal. But I was a little concerned that it might be too cold and a bit clinical.

I saw my opportunity in a corner, where I could squeeze in a breakfast table. There's always something cozy about a table in a kitchen. It feels warm and intimate, and sometimes you just want to cook something and sit down and eat it right there.

I could have done something modern, but frankly I already had enough modern with the Bulthaup cabinets. And anyway, modern—with all its hard edges—always looks slightly odd to me in London. The city is just too steeped in the past for cutting-edge modern to really work for me here. So I decided to take the same aesthetic but push it in a slightly different direction. I made the table more 1930s Streamline Moderne, to romanticize it a bit. With its dark mahogany top and metallic edge, it looks like something you might see on a yacht—or an upscale diner (I realize that may be a contradiction in terms). I did a banquette and two chairs to accompany it and upholstered them in burnt yellow fabric, because I wanted that flash of color in the gray London light.

I found some interesting pillows and covered the little bit of wall space I had in a textured wallpaper by Elizabeth Dow. But the one piece that really makes that corner, and the room, is a seventeenth-century Italian sunburst mirror. And the uncanny thing about it is that it looks as if it could have come straight out of the 1950s. It's a wild, eye-catching delight that functions almost like a piece of jewelry. It brings the sun into that corner and livens up the whole space.

If you want to humanize a kitchen, you can do it with a few well-chosen accessories, but the real secret is the social component. You want to make room for people, because that's when conversation happens and you get all that life. There was already a window seat here, but I made it even more inviting with a cushion and pillows, so you could really relax and be comfortable. Or friends could sit down and keep the host company while he's cooking. The more seating you have in a kitchen, the more time you are likely to spend there, because people will be drawn to a space where they can eat and drink and sit around and talk.

A breakfast area adds a little color and warmth to a modern kitchen. The chairs and the banquette are upholstered in Marouquin Jaune by Manuel Canovas. Isn't it interesting how that photograph of Versailles by Robert Polidori makes the space feel bigger? The wall practically evaporates, and you feel as if you're looking into another room. The crosshatched wall covering is by Elizabeth Dow. I found that great faceted 1930s-style ceiling fixture at Charles Edwards in London.

Wouldn't it be lovely
to stretch out on that
window seat in the
morning sun with a cup
of tea? That's what that
little round table is
there for, to hold your
drink and your phone. It
also throws in a few
curves next to all those
straight-laced lines. It's by
Soane, and it reminds me
of a chess piece. The
rolling cart could follow
you to another room,
with a pot of tea and the
newspapers. It's also
by Soane, in that soft
nickel finish I love.

FIFTH AVENUE, MANHATTAN

I t's very challenging to design a space and make it feel modern and luxurious at the same time. Especially when all you have to start with is an empty shell in a Manhattan high rise.

But this apartment had two major advantages. It was on a very high floor overlooking Central Park and there were windows in every direction, so you felt as if you were living in the sky. The light and the views were extraordinary. That's the most wonderful thing about being in a building like this, and we didn't even try to pretend that we were anywhere else. So what if the rooms were basically a series of boxes?

No problem. We would turn them into the most beautiful boxes you had ever seen. Each would have its own particular feeling and together they would tell a story and create a sense of history and romance. It would be a new kind of elegance, combining past and present with a twenty-first-century attitude. I wanted it to be sensual and surprising. Anything could go into the mix. There were no rules and no boundaries.

The most clean, cool, almost minimal box is the kitchen. The cabinetry is a geometric composition of pure planes with no visible hardware to interrupt the white lacquer finish. It makes me think of an iceberg. Yet somehow it's not cold, because it reflects the light. Next to it, the stainless steel appliances look like molten silver. There's a gray-green granite on the countertops and *pietra serena* stone on the floor, which somehow feels ancient and modern at the same time. It may be a simple kitchen, but it's definitely not plain.

With its immaculate Bulthaup cabinetry, the kitchen feels a bit like a Bauhaus laboratory. The cabinets are very well constructed and finished in a high-performance lacquer. A pair of pen-and-ink drawings by Willem de Kooning near the sink is framed in silver to catch the light. The ceiling fixtures are by Jean Perzel, a German designer who worked in France in the 1920s and 1930s and became famous for his art deco lights.

In an apartment that is all about rare and unusual finishes, this dressing room and bath done for the wife may be the most exquisite. It is all about atmosphere, and was inspired by a famous bathroom that the French designer Armand-Albert Rateau did for the couturier Jeanne Lanvin back in the 1920s. The two rooms look nothing alike. All they have in common is a concept—the bath as a piece of jewelry.

Gold is the theme, and I used three different colors of gold tile—a gold, a white gold, and a rose gold—on the walls around the tub. It's like a modern version of the Byzantine mosaics made of shimmering gold tile on the ceilings of St. Mark's Basilica in Venice. In the dressing room, I commissioned the artist Nancy Lorenz to cover the walls and closet doors in squares of gold leaf. If you look closely, you'll see they are also inlaid with mother-of-pearl in a design that resembles one of Buckminster Fuller's geodesic domes. Ancient and modern combine, once again. The effect is dazzling.

ABOVE LEFT: There's a dressing table tucked into a niche beside the gold-leafed closet doors, which gleam in the light. The French chandeliers are like a pair of pavé diamond earrings, but in this case they're made of rock crystal. ABOVE RIGHT: The hexagonal vanity is also gold-leafed, and the knobs on the door—and the handles of my Town faucet—are made of rock crystal. OPPOSITE: The bath is worthy of Gustav Klimt. That amazing mirror was made in the 1940s and once belonged to the great American decorator Rose Cumming. The gold Davlin tiles on the walls are by Ann Sacks.

Each bathroom is completely different, and as you walk in, you feel as if you've stepped inside a jewel box. It's a heady sensation, to be enveloped in these rich and strange materials.

Straw marquetry and shagreen. Those are two materials I rarely get to use, so it was a glorious indulgence to play with them in these two bathrooms.

You might as well go all out in a powder room. This is the place to do something over the top because you don't have that much square footage to deal with. So I decided to cover the walls in straw marquetry. It's a centuries-old technique that very few people know how to do these days. It's meant to mimic wood marquetry, and in order to get the varying shades from pale gold to dark brown that you'd see in a wood veneer, you use wheat or oat straw and then soak it in cold, warm, or hot water. Finally it's ironed and then glued down. Trust me, it's not something you want to try at home. It's very time-consuming and labor-intensive.

Then I hung a glazed stoneware mirror by artist Eve Kaplan that looks like something that came out of a cave. I love the contrast—the rough and the smooth, the primitive and the refined. It makes a bold statement.

In the husband's bathroom, I went for a totally different mood. The walls are sheathed in a figured green marble outlined in blue-green limestone. It has kind of an undersea quality. Then the vanity is made of pale green shagreen and inset with a bronze sink. Right opposite, there's a painting of London Bridge at night that reminds me of James McNeil Whistler's *Nocturne*. It's all in murky tones of black and blue and green and gray. The room feels dark and masculine, and was influenced by a bathroom at Barbara Hutton's Winfield House, which is now the official residence of the American ambassador to England.

OPPOSITE: Ask me why I did a bronze vanity with a stone top. Why not? The sconces are by contemporary artist Hervé Van der Straeten. The straw marquetry was made for us in Paris by Féau & Cie, the amazing craftsmen who also make all my boiserie. ABOVE: At the back of the husband's bath is a large, open shower with a window that looks out on Fifth Avenue.

Marble is an amazing material. It can feel solid and weighty or light and ethereal. Each type has its own character and adds instant personality to a room.

I was mesmerized by this Turkish marble that looks almost like a pinstripe, or old-fashioned ribbon candy, or a waterfall in blue and gray and white, and used it on the walls in a guest bath. Notice how each slab is perfectly aligned, as if we were matching wallpaper, to create a continuous line. The vertical stripe is contrasted by a dark gray stone on all the horizontal planes—the tub surround and the countertop on the vanity and the tiles on the floor. Together they create a very tailored look. It's crisp and clean and to me, it feels almost neoclassical. You walk into the bathroom and feel as if you're in a Napoleonic campaign tent, but made of marble instead of cloth. The pattern seduces the eye and suggests all sorts of stories.

ABOVE: The mirrors in the guest bathroom expand the space and make you feel as if you're wrapped in the cityscape. OPPOSITE: The mirror above my Town tub for Kallista was made in Paris of patinated metal and brings even more light into the bath. I chose the gray stone for the floor and countertops because it calms down the striped Asher marble, from Ann Sacks, and balances the composition.

BEL AIR, CALIFORNIA

This is a 1920s house with a fine pedigree—it was built by the English architect Gordon Kaufmann, who also designed the turreted Greystone mansion for the oil-rich Doheny family. It's a prime example of the vaguely Mediterranean style so popular at the time, with a grand central hall, spacious rooms, and tall French doors opening to the garden. But by the time my clients bought it, most of the interior details were long gone, replaced by mirrors and track lighting.

So architect Oscar Shamamian and I did that Ralph Lauren thing, reinventing and reimagining it in a way that brought back all its traditional charm and even made it a little more hip and interesting. The kitchen is a fantasy—an idealized version of the kind of staff kitchen you'd see in one of those Gatsby-esque mansions on the Gold Coast of Long Island, where Sabrina lived in the chauffeur's quarters above the garage. It's all white and crisp and clean, with glazed subway tiles on the backsplash and creamy statuary marble on the counters and white-painted wood cupboards that go all the way up to the ceiling.

We chose the hardware very carefully. In a kitchen, it's the equivalent of jewelry. It sets the tone and you can also use it to date a space. Here, the old-fashioned thumb turns and butterfly hinges instantly take you back to the turn of the century. In the old days, this would have been the servants' domain and the family would rarely, if ever, have ventured into it. The cook would have been summoned to meet with the mistress of the house on her side of the swinging door, to plan the meals.

But today, we've erased all those boundaries. The owners of the house are just as likely to be doing their own cooking, and the stools at the island are there for family and friends, so they can be part of the activity. That's why one side of the island is raised, to bring it up to a comfortable height for eating at the counter. The extra height also means you don't have to look at stacks of dirty dishes from the other side of the room, where there's a breakfast table.

It's fascinating to trace how the kitchen has gradually evolved over the decades into a family room. It's a new paradigm. But what's interesting here is how it still retains connotations of the old servants' domain. People just like that look. It reminds us of a more genteel time and makes us all feel like we're living in a movie.

The countertops are made of Calcutta Gold marble, which I like because it's creamier than Carrara. It looks like melted vanilla ice cream. The hardware is made of nickel and so are the light fixtures, which are from Urban Archaeology. The stools are by Ann-Morris Antiques.

Gatsby would have loved the husband's dressing room. I can just see all those beautiful shirts spread out on the leather top of the packing island, which is made of mahogany. The vaulted ceiling and the paneled walls that Oscar designed are worthy of a robber baron. The room feels almost like a library.

The mood in the wife's bathroom is very different—more grand hotel in Biarritz. The colors are all cream and white, which makes it feel light and ethereal. The Paris tub from Water Monopoly is a reproduction of an early twentieth-century French tub that was originally made in fireclay. This one has the same curvaceous rim, but it's done in a composite material so it's half the weight. I bought the mirror over the tub because I liked its shape, and the marble frame is unusual. It adds to the ceremonial aspect of the bath. Everything feels pure and pristine. There's nothing jarring here—and no reminders of the twenty-first century to interrupt the reverie.

ABOVE LEFT: A glorious Venetian mirror has such beautiful lines that it almost qualifies as architecture. It adds a sense of richness to this powder room. ABOVE RIGHT: In the wife's bath, Regent sconces in polished nickel from Ann-Morris Antiques provide a soft light. The faucets and hand shower are by Lefroy Brooks. OPPOSITE: The husband's dressing room feels very masculine with all the mahogany furniture and paneling. But then there's the surprise of that vaulted ceiling, painted a celestial blue. Hanging from the very center is a nineteenth-century bronze light fixture, made in France, which once burnt oil and has now been electrified.

In its heyday in the 1930s, the Hollywood Regency style was the epitome of chic. It took the classic English look and tweaked it with more streamlined furniture and a touch of chinoiserie. Architects like James Dolena, who built this house, knew how to create camera-ready interiors that looked as if they were just waiting for Joan Crawford and George Cukor to show up and start filming.

Someone had renovated this house in the 1980s and created this huge kitchen and family-room area that was a little more loftlike and modern than the house wanted to be. Architect Oscar Shamamian and I kept the volume and the space, but we redid it to feel more traditional and cozy. We added old-fashioned glass cabinets with beautiful nickel knobs to flank the great big window that overlooks the garden. The kitchen is still open to the family room, but now the two spaces are separated in a subtle way, divided by an island that, on the family-room side, becomes a bookcase. Then there's a massive bronze hood above the cooktop on the island that has a very Regency, Royal-Pavilion-at-Brighton kind of shape. It does a really effective job of making you aware that these are two distinctive areas with different functions, without closing off either of them.

You see a lot of the kitchen from the living area, but it doesn't get in the way. The tile backsplash and the painted cupboards are the creamy color of a magnolia blossom, elegant and simple and properly self-effacing. When the alabaster lights are dimmed to a glow, you could forget that there's a kitchen there entirely.

ABOVE: There's a neat little grill embedded in the countertop, which is great for bringing out the flavor of vegetables and meat. OPPOSITE: The counters are made of Botticino limestone with a classic bullnose edge, which is dressier than the typical right angle. The faucet is from my Town collection for Kallista. The alabaster light fixtures are by Charles Edwards. FOLLOWING SPREAD: A big square coffee table anchors the seating area. Anyone cooking at the stove looks out into the room and can be part of the conversation.

The room is zoned into different areas. A large bay on one side was the perfect place for a breakfast table. The furniture in the seating area has a typically English look, with a sofa covered in tobacco-colored linen velvet and an easy chair slipcovered in chintz. A pair of suede-covered benches sit on the side closest to the fireplace. The room has such a clear center, marked by the coffee table and the Oriental rug, and that's where the large pieces of furniture land. I didn't want anything too big and bulky by that wall of glass. I want you to see that view. The huge windows make the room feel as if it's part of the garden.

You can see right through the fretwork on the Chinese Chippendale-style chairs, which makes them work particularly well by that window. They also fit right in with the Brighton Pavilion spirit. They're charming and whimsical, but you still have to take them seriously because the lines are so strong. That's a very appealing combination.

ABOVE: The apron check on the shades warms up the wide expanse of glass and has a casual kitchen-y feel. OPPOSITE: The hanging lamp by Charles Edwards is understated and not at all fussy. The large round shade echoes the shape of the breakfast table and helps to define the space. I bought the Chinese Chippendale-style chairs in London and left them in their original leather seats.

These Hollywood Regency–style houses have one foot in the modern age, but they're still incurably romantic. That's why I went with "pretty" in the master bathroom. It suits the spirit.

Can't you just see Norma Shearer putting on her lipstick at that dressing table? This is a very elegant room, but it still has a sense of theatricality. The tub is at center stage, in front of a large window that overlooks the garden. It's flanked by two towers of open shelves, which hold enough fluffy white towels to dry off the whole cast of *The Women*.

Actually, this is a relatively small space that we reworked into a dressing room as well, with closets opposite the tub beyond the mirrors. There really isn't much wall space, so we decided to make the most of what is there, with a stripe painted in two shades of seafoam green. It's a lovely Robert Adam sort of color.

Billy Haines, an actor turned decorator who did the interiors of some of the most famous Hollywood Regency houses, loved to buy for clients like Joan Crawford in England. There's an Anglophile aspect to many of these rooms. Who could resist lovely European furniture like that caned chair? I bought it at Colefax and Fowler in London. It's so pretty, painted in that pale shade of green and cushioned in chintz. It's the kind of thing you'd find on a George Cukor set at MGM, or in his own home, which was designed by James Dolena and decorated by Billy Haines. These three men were all instrumental in creating the Hollywood Regency style. Once it made its way to the movie screen, the rest of the interior design world picked up on it. Movies and design have always been inextricably entwined. It's hard to say sometimes which came first. Did the trend start on the street or on the screen? It works both ways, and they influence each other.

ABOVE: A Swedish chair by the dressing table has that beautifully worn paint, which adds such a lovely patina to the room. OPPOSITE: The tub looks more like a piece of furniture when it's encased in cabinetry. The surround is made of Botticino limestone. The shower is at the end of the room, just to the left of the towel rack.

*If you want to create a lovely
romantic atmosphere, find a good
old-fashioned English chintz.*

    Can't you practically smell the lilacs? I love this old Colefax and Fowler chintz, and I covered the walls of a guest bathroom in it. I wanted you to feel completely enveloped. It's one of those patterns with a beautiful foreground and background—you feel as if you are looking through the lilac branches, in a way. And there's something about chintz that immediately transports me back to the 1920s and 1930s and all those great English country houses decorated by women like Sibyl Colefax and Nancy Lancaster. Lancaster became a partner in Colefax and Fowler after Sibyl Colefax retired, and worked closely with John Fowler on her own projects. She brought a fresh American eye to those stuffy English houses and frankly outdid the English at their own look.

    When you open the door to this bathroom, you feel as if you are walking into a garden. It's the prettiest room. Everything in it has a certain delicacy, including the washstand, with its slim glass legs balanced on brass feet. Above the sink is a seventeenth-century chinoiserie mirror with a cushion frame, which means the wood is curved like a cushion. We also hung some vintage Chinese paintings done on silk. The lighting is part of the mood. The candlestick sconces with tiny lamp shades help to convince you that you're in another era. Yet they're timeless as well. Like a beautiful floral chintz, they never really go out of style.

We took a washstand by Urban Archaeology and customized it with an octagonal top made
of Carrara marble. The veining has the same random wandering-vine quality as the pattern
in the chintz, and they seemed to go well together. The Ritz faucets are by P. E. Guerin.

COUNTRY

PARADISE VALLEY, ARIZONA

When you live in the Arizona desert, you alternate between basking in the sun and retreating from it. My clients, working with architect Don Ziebell, built a house with thick stone walls and a red tile roof that could be in the south of France or a hill town in Tuscany—until you look more closely at the nearby hills and realize that they're dotted with cactus plants, not olive trees.

The idea behind the house is that it's both open to the outdoors—with French doors in every room—and a fortress against the scorching heat. That's because those foot-thick walls are not just decorative. They keep the rooms cool. In the kitchen, we walked the same fine line between open and enclosed because we wanted natural light, but it was important to be able to control it. A bank of casement windows by the door to the terrace can be opened to the breeze, but if the sun gets too bright, the linen shades can be pulled down.

The vertically striped shades balance the horizontal bank of windows and make the room feel crisp and clean. Stripes are a motif that appears in many European cultures. The brass faucets look vaguely French. The stone mantel on the hood over the range could be Italian. So where does the idea of Arizona come into the design? Well, it's not overt, but subtle. You see it in the colors of the room, which are taken from the landscape. The Costa Esmeralda marble on the island and countertops is a sage green. The walls and the cabinetry are a sandy cream. And the copper farmhouse sink has a nice weathered patina that hints of the mines and pioneer times and seems to suit the location.

A skylight is positioned over the island, because this is where you really need light as you prepare a meal. And there's something almost primeval about an island with a pool of light on it. We're all essentially nomadic creatures and we're drawn to this modern version of a campfire. It becomes the heart of the house and gives the kitchen a glow. Then I like to top things off with a hanging pot rack. I use this particular one, by Ann-Morris Antiques, over and over again because it's so good-looking and supremely functional. You can see all your pots at a glance and just unhook the one you want. I also like the way the pots mask the artificial light source. You can still see the pendant lights but they're not the first thing your eye focuses on. It's always more interesting when the source of light in a room remains a little mysterious.

Rough-hewn posts and beams frame a view of Camelback Mountain from the outdoor dining terrace. The wicker chairs around the table are by Ralph Lauren Home. FOLLOWING SPREAD: Like a canopy over a bed, the hanging pot rack defines the island as the focal point of the kitchen. Three people can perch on stools at one end, where the overhang offers enough room for their legs so they can be comfortable. The island is outfitted with a KitchenAid microwave and a prep sink by Kallista. The copper sink is by Rocky Mountain Hardware. The faucets are by Waterworks. The drawer pulls were made in France by Bouvet. And I chose a BlueStar Heritage Classic range—with a professional-style raised griddle and broiler—because I have one at home and I love it.

A fireplace suggests the idea of cooking on the hearth, and architect Don Ziebell cleverly elevated it so you can see the flames when you're sitting at the dining table. A lime wash lightens the stone and makes it look almost sun-bleached. I had the table made out of old wood and was very lucky to find a set of late eighteenth-century Italian chairs that have the right scale and are amazingly comfortable.

The boundaries between inside and outside seem to dissolve when the huge steel-framed doors are left open to the desert air. You can bathe in the tub or you can shower outdoors in a private courtyard.

There are days in Arizona when the air is dry and crisp and the sun feels delightfully warm on your skin and there really seems no reason to go inside. And that's when a room like this is bliss. Just open all the French doors to the private courtyard, and it's the next best thing to bathing outdoors.

I love the shape of that tub. It's a classic French bateau, taller and therefore deeper than an American tub so when you lean back, the water actually covers your shoulders. Heaven. Really, all you need is that tub and you're home free, design-wise, because it's like a piece of sculpture in the room.

I kept everything else very simple. Soft white curtains, made of a Ralph Lauren fabric with a barely-there stripe, stitched together so it looks like a large-scale seersucker. The wallcovering by Elizabeth Dow also has a subtle stripe, which adds more texture to the room. A beautiful antique silver chandelier was wired for electricity and can be dimmed, to give off the gentlest light. I chose the little Berber rug because it picks up the colors of the desert.

The Empire tub by Water Monopoly is beautifully designed, with the curve at your back sized just to fit your shoulders. The faucet and hand-held shower by Waterworks is made of brass, with wood handles. That small rustic touch is a nod to the setting. I designed the étagère for Jasper, my own line, and it's just the right size for toiletries and a few towels. FOLLOWING SPREAD: His-and-hers dressing rooms are connected by this shared space, furnished with a nineteenth-century chaise upholstered in a new linen check. You can sit down and be comfortable as you put on your shoes. The kids can also hang out while their parents are getting dressed for a party.

MILLBROOK, NEW YORK

You can see for miles from the hilltop where this house now stands. It's a view straight out of an American pastoral painting, with rolling hills and dense forests and a blur of mountains in the distance. When my clients couldn't find a great old house on the kind of property they wanted, with enough room for horses and paddocks and stables, they decided to build their own. But it was very important to them that it not look like a brand-new suburban mansion. This is a horse farm, with stallions grazing on the grass between white picket fences. And the kind of home they envisioned was a rambling farmhouse that would feel as if it had always been part of the land.

Gil Schafer was the architect and he did a brilliant job, designing a traditional center-hall Colonial with a few significant differences. It had higher ceilings and larger rooms and every modern convenience—things you could never get in an old house—and yet it still felt as if it truly were old. I guess you could say he had a head start, because the clients actually bought a late eighteenth-century house in a neighboring town and took it apart, salvaging the floorboards and the beams and all the period details to reuse here. We wanted that patina, and when we didn't have it, we tried to recreate it.

We all have an idea in our head about what an eighteenth-century house should look like, but that doesn't necessarily mean we're actually prepared to live in one. Some people like the idea better than the reality, and besides, I'm not all that interested in building authentic period rooms. I'll leave that to the museums.

Often, it turns out that all you need to create the mood is a suggestion. The family room, which is part of an enclosed porch just off the kitchen, is a case in point. You would probably not see floor-to-ceiling windows and a 10-foot ceiling in a real eighteenth-century farmhouse. It would have been way too hard to heat. But because the ceiling is supported with old beams and the floorboards are made of reclaimed wood, you buy into the illusion. Plus, a few good American primitive pieces, like the old painted table by the window and that beautifully carved comb-back Windsor chair, create such a strong impression that the whole room feels equally antique.

A wicker sofa is one of those quintessentially American pieces of furniture that says, "Come sit right down and relax." We painted the ceiling blue, because that's a traditional color for porches. Some people say it wards off bugs and prevents wasps from building their nests because it fools them into thinking it's the sky. Actually, it was probably the lye in the old milk paint that repelled them. In any event, it's a calming color and connects the room to the view outside.

This is a farmhouse kitchen, but scaled up in size to accommodate all the guests who fill the house on country weekends. Everybody can gather here on Sunday morning and help make coffee and flip pancakes.

The kitchen is picturesque, with whitewashed beams and old wood floors and hollyhock chintz on the window shades, but it's also very hard-working. The countertops are made of flamed black granite, which has a rough, worn texture and the darkness of age. The stone seems to relate to the countryside and also turns out to be very durable. It doesn't show stains.

There are two sinks, which is always useful because it means you have two zones, one for prep on the island and another for washing dishes. The primary sink is one of those classic Shaws Original farmhouse sinks made out of fireclay. It doesn't stain and it can stand up to all sorts of abuse. You can even scour it without worrying about leaving marks. It's practically indestructible.

Gil designed carved wooden brackets to support the upper cabinets, which makes them feel more old-fashioned. Then we added country-style L-shaped strap hinges made of black iron, the kind of thing you might see in a barn or a tack room. And we used restoration glass in the cupboard doors, so they would look even older. A very practical stainless steel backsplash fills the gap between the 60-inch dual-fuel Wolf range and the hood. I always pay particular attention to the hood, because it's one of the largest elements in a kitchen and it instantly telegraphs character. This one looks like a relic of the early industrial age. It's made of distressed zinc, which has been blackened to make it look as if it has seen the smoke of hundreds of fires.

ABOVE: A white farmhouse sink, made of fireclay in the traditional way, always looks clean, especially against flamed black granite countertops. It's paired with my Town faucet in a soft nickel finish. The beadboard on the walls adds to the old-fashioned look.
OPPOSITE: I love this pot rack by Ann-Morris Antiques and use it every chance I get. It's utilitarian and has such a nice heft. There's something very appealing about those hooks, which look serious and remind me of the kind of meat hooks you see at the butcher's.

I wanted you to feel as if you were back in the eighteenth-century and this was a room that had just been converted into a bath. But luckily you don't have to lug buckets of hot water up from the fireplace. The one piece of furniture in the room has the impact of a piece of sculpture. It's a beautiful antique English chair shaped like an hourglass.

If you choose your plumbing carefully, it can help you create atmosphere. These fixtures are not old but they have a lovely antique look.

It's more interesting to go beyond the basic function of a bath and try to create a sense of place and history and mood. In the eighteenth century, rooms were relatively spare, so I had to accomplish all this with only a few gestures. It started with those beautiful wide-plank floors. If you go to the trouble of having a real, authentic floor, then you need a real, authentic carpet. This Khotan rug is worn and flattened and has clearly lived through a lifetime or two. If you had a fluffy white rug in here, it just wouldn't convey the same feeling.

Stripes are a traditional eighteenth-century motif and this striped wallpaper by Elizabeth Dow is handpainted, which makes it feel antique. You would never have smooth Sheetrock walls in an old house. I needed that bit of texture. The tub is freestanding and has echoes of an old-fashioned hip bath. Whenever you pull a tub away from the wall, it immediately makes a bathroom feel older.

Every piece of furniture does not have to be historically accurate. The washstands with their glass legs are a twist on an eighteenth-century commode, which would often have a marble top. Here they look so light and airy that they almost vanish. The mirrors above are surrounded with a faux-grained wood frame. Faux graining was very common in the eighteenth-century, to make a simple wood like pine or oak look more like mahogany. These mirrors conveniently hide the medicine cabinets. Be sure to choose light fixtures that enhance the period effect. It's easy to imagine that the antique sconces flanking the mirrors are still holding candles.

ABOVE: I love the glass legs on this washstand by Urban Archaeology. There are two, on opposite sides of the room. They look so ethereal that they almost disappear. OPPOSITE: The tub and fixtures are from my Town collection for Kallista. A sort of suspension of disbelief occurs when you see the old-fashioned standing waste pipe rising out of the old wood floor. It takes you back to another century.

There's something innately charming about a room tucked under the eaves. It's like a found space, with all the nooks and crannies you'd expect in an old house. This guest bath is up on the third floor and the window by the tub is low to the ground because it's geared to the sloping roofline, and the architectural proportions of the house as seen from outside. That makes for a delightfully quirky space inside.

We played up that eccentricity by painting the antique tub a bayberry green. It makes it more special and unusual. The soft, dark color kind of recedes, and somehow the whole bathroom feels quieter. Nothing here is built-in. The tub is free-standing. There's no vanity with wooden doors. All I wanted was a simple pedestal sink, made of creamy white porcelain.

If you needed a place to store something back then, you brought in a piece of furniture. I found a nineteenth-century English cabinet made of bamboo and put it in the corner, to hold towels. It's the kind of thing that was very popular during the Victorian era—a touch of Chinoiserie to add a little whimsy to the room. And there's something casual and impromptu about a dark piece of furniture in a light room. It's as if you just pulled it in there out of necessity, with no particular thought about matching anything. The room feels lived in, which is different than decorated.

The muted colors and old-fashioned patterns of the ticking stripe at the windows and the nineteenth-century American hooked rug on the floor also contribute to the feeling of age. The pedestal sink and toilet are from my Town collection and the faucets and fixtures are from my Country collection, both for Kallista.

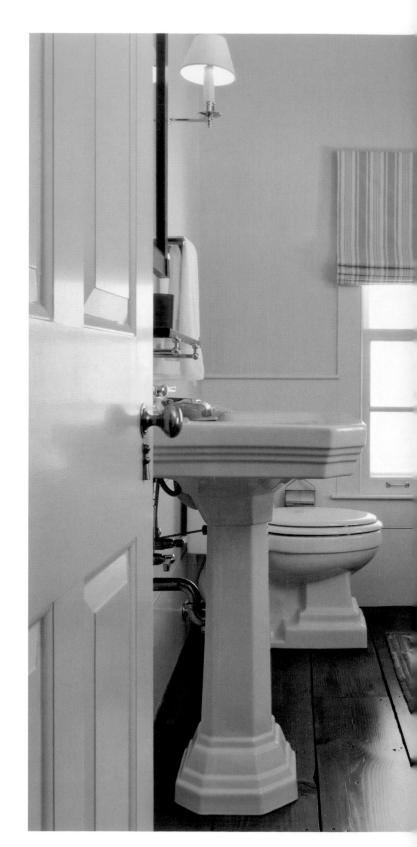

BIG SKY, MONTANA

Forget the antlers and the American Indian blankets. You're not going to see any of those typical log cabin trappings here. I didn't want this to be just like every other house on the mountain, with raw wood and twig tables everywhere you look.

The aesthetic here is a little harder to pin down. You still get a sense of being in nature when you sit down at the simple Nakashima-style table in the dining room. But it's surrounded by elegant leather chairs that would look equally at home in an apartment on the Left Bank. And the wrought-iron chandelier resembles something by Giacometti, rather than a wagon wheel.

I'm not interested in conjuring up the old West. This is a vacation house, where the family comes to ski in the winter, but they didn't want to turn it into a theme park. It has a more contemporary point of view, with a wide range of furnishings. Various ideas and periods coexist. The clients bought the house while it was under construction, and we took down a few walls to give it a more open plan. Now the dining room and the kitchen and the breakfast area are all one big space.

I used a few old-fashioned elements in the kitchen to add a little homespun charm. The tin ceiling takes you back to another century. The glass-fronted cabinets, painted a barn red, could have come straight out of a general store. I chose Windsor chairs and benches to go around the breakfast table because they have that simple, sturdy Early American integrity. But the combined effect is just to inflect it with some American roots. It does not feel like a period room. It looks very welcoming and warm. There's no confusion about what era you're in when you're sitting at that cantilevered breakfast bar. You can drink your coffee and look out at the mountains through the tall banks of windows. After all, you've come all the way out here to be closer to nature. I never want you to forget where you are.

The elements are simple—wood, leather, iron—but put together in a way that feels contemporary rather than log cabin. The chairs in the foreground are by the Mexican architect Luis Barragan and were bought at auction. I designed the Jazz armchairs around the table for my Jasper collection. They're done in saddle leather and modeled after a late-1920s, early-1930s French chair I found. I loved the beautifully tapered legs.

The stone on the countertops relates to the stone you see outside. This kitchen is large enough to include two comfortable seating areas—a breakfast bar and a family-size table in front of the view. The island in the center is topped with wood and offers a great big work surface and plenty of storage.

This is a ski house and the couple who own it could easily have twenty people staying with them, but when they want to get away from it all they can retreat to the master bath, which is like a small private spa. I've seen bathtubs in the middle of the room in some chic Parisian hotels, and this is kind of the same idea. Life goes on in and around the tub.

Here, the bathroom seems to have morphed into a sitting room, with a sofa and chairs and a coffee table by the tub (there's also a fireplace and a TV). The couple could sit and talk and have some quiet time together, while one of them is relaxing in the tub. The tub is set into a niche and lined with a backsplash made of one of those dark limestones that I love. The same limestone forms the vanities. There are two of them, on opposite walls. The dark stone is a nice contrast to the paler Venetian plaster. The floor is made of wood, which is warm underfoot and seems to suit a house in the mountains. People are often resistant to a wood floor in a bath but it's fine, as long as you don't leave a couple gallons of water on the floor and walk away for two days.

There's a wonderful rug by Charles Voysey on the floor, which does a lot to warm up the room. He was a leading architect and designer in England during the Arts & Crafts period. The coffee table is a vintage Japanese piece. The lantern is by Paul Ferrante.

SANTA YNEZ, CALIFORNIA

Are we really in California? The view over the vineyards looks remarkably like the Tuscan hills, and the house is a Mediterranean-style villa that could be mistaken for the country estate of a family from Rome. So of course the kitchen had to have that same warm, Italian atmosphere.

It starts with the terra-cotta tile floors and the barnlike ceiling. The voluminous scale of the space makes it seem as if this could be an outbuilding that was converted into a kitchen. Everything in the room needed to be equally big. The island is a huge slab of butcher block resting on a wooden top that's a foot thick. A gigantic cabinet—part armoire and part confessional—divides the cooking area from the pantry area and also conceals the Sub-Zero refrigerator. Mark Rios, the architect, came up with that idea, and it works very well. I like how it stops—with a strong cornice line that brings the room down to a more human scale—instead of going all the way up to the ceiling. It's also much more powerful to keep that beautiful ceiling plane unbroken.

You know how in Tuscany the light is somehow more golden than in other places? It has this hazy, amber quality, and I tried to re-create it with my palette of materials. The range has a copper hood, which adds instant warmth. And it doesn't bother me that the range itself is made of stainless steel. Not every metal has to match. Actually, it makes me think of those weird Italian espresso machines that are the size of a small car and concocted out of copper, brass, and stainless steel and topped with an eagle.

The countertops are honed Botticino limestone, which carries its own glow. And then you have all that rich wood, and copper pots hanging on the wall, and sunlight streaming through the windows. It makes me want to sit down and dig into a plate of pasta.

A pergola draped with wisteria and dotted with Iceberg roses frames a view of the mountains just beyond the vineyards and the man-made pond. Dwarf olive trees are planted in terra-cotta pots. Thyme, isotoma, and mint add a scent to the breeze and flourish in between the pavers. The wrought-iron chairs and sofas are by Janus et Cie and are covered in burgundy Sunbrella indoor-outdoor fabric.

This is not a display kitchen but a place where you can really cook, as evidenced by all the oils and condiments within arm's reach by the range. A good selection of knives is nearby, along with canisters of flour and pasta and all the things you use every day. The Holophane lights may not be strictly Italian, but they give off a great, strong light, which is especially important in this loftlike room. The round elmwood table in the foreground is from Quatrain. The chairs are antique Italian, bought in Parma, and slipcovered in a simple gingham check—La Seyne by Brunschwig & Fils—as they might have done in the eighteenth century.

I took several rooms and turned them into this palatial bath, which feels like something you'd find only in Europe. The tub is the focal point, and it's encased in slabs of Rouge Royal limestone. It's the most extraordinary shade of red, very Italian and earthy, and it seems particularly appropriate to this house, which is part of a winery. And I needed all that space underneath the stone because it's a Jacuzzi tub and we had to hide the mechanism. (Full disclosure: the marble surround didn't have to be *quite* that big. We pumped it up for effect.) And then we added that elegantly shaped backsplash, which conjures up another era and gives the tub a certain formality.

It's not often that you have a fireplace in a bathroom, but when you do, you should take full advantage of it. I flanked this one with two inviting armchairs, covered in an Etro damask in a gorgeous carnelian red that echoes the stone around the tub. The fabric has a sheen but isn't shiny, which is the way I prefer it. The sink against the back wall is a mini version of the tub, surrounded with the same limestone. Red is the dominant color here, red and the burnt butterscotch color of the Venetian plaster walls. The two shades combine in the checked silk curtains. The lamp shades on the sconces are the same color as the walls, which is all about making the light softer and more romantic.

The pale limestone floor is cool to the feet on a hot summer day and decorated with a tiny mosaic border. I don't usually hang oil paintings over tubs, but this was a special circumstance. It's flanked by marble samples that I had framed—an easy idea that looks a lot more expensive than it is.

MARTHA'S VINEYARD, MASSACHUSETTS

There's something about the Vineyard that feels very New England Yankee to me. I think of it as simple and basic, grounded in the rock and the soil and the rhythms of the sea. It's different from the Hamptons—less fancy, more rustic. You don't see a lot of perfectly groomed boxwood hedges, just old, rambling walls made of dry-stacked stones.

Oscar Shamamian was the architect who designed the house, and I enjoy working with him because we think the same way. As we were discussing what it should look like, we had this image in our heads, kind of a cross between the House of the Seven Gables and an old fishing shack—weathered shingles, dark green trim—so it would seem as if it were part of the landscape.

I thought the kitchen should feel very utilitarian. No-nonsense, like the people who live here. But I didn't want it to look like a staff kitchen. There are no servants toiling away out of sight. It's more of a country kitchen, where the family can get into the act of preparing their own food. You go out in the morning to pick blueberries and then come in here to make a cobbler for dessert. I could imagine the man of the house striding in with a fishing creel over his shoulder. He catches the fish. He cleans the fish.

And I didn't see it as white and bright, like every other kitchen today. Instead, I wanted it to be more moody, and color can do that. We painted the cabinets and the trim in a murky green, not unlike the exterior trim on the house. The soft, dark shade adds age. So do the wide floorboards, made of reclaimed oak. There's a big farmhouse sink with a built-in drain board, one of my designs for Kallista, and an unpretentious faucet that looks as if it could have been here for decades. The countertops are dark as well, made of Lagos Azul limestone that shows a few marks, which doesn't bother me because those are another sign of age. I chose handmade tiles for the backsplash because they have such a nice patina; there are places where the glaze is gone and you see the bisque underneath. That feels more earthy, and it reminds me of American art pottery done around the turn of the century.

This is a working kitchen, with pots and pans in full view on a shelf under the island. Above it, we hung old lights with brass trim that look as if they could have come off a fishing vessel, and we painted them green too. The hood over the range is not made of shiny metal: it's a dark, tarnished zinc. Little things, like the carved brackets under the upper cabinets, contribute to the old-fashioned feeling. And those cabinets have sliding glass-paned doors, a detail you see in many nineteenth-century butler's pantries. Know what? It turns out to be very practical, because you don't have all those doors opening out and getting in the way.

The Shingle Style house by the sea is a fine old American tradition. And a summer day on the Vineyard is perfect for dining outdoors. Lloyd Loom wicker chairs, another classic, surround the table. FOLLOWING SPREAD: The kitchen is down-home and "dirt country" rather than fancy. In early American houses, you often see dark trim on light walls, and that's what we did here. You could sit in that Windsor chair and shuck corn. If the family is having a big dinner party and somebody else is cooking, pocket doors can close off the pass-through, which is just to the left of the door to the dining room. We call it the Mary Tyler Moore window.

The master bath is tucked under the eaves. It's a nice-size room, with a vintage tub that has been re-enameled and set by the window. It's interesting—a freestanding tub always makes a bathroom feel more antique, as if it were once a bedroom or a study that was only adapted to this new use with the advent of indoor plumbing. And Oscar and I like to build in little eccentricities, like the sharply angled door. Those kinds of things make a house feel old rather than new.

You can soak in the tub and look out at the ocean. When the windows are open, you get a lovely sea breeze that sends the linen shades wafting back and forth. It's a calm room because the colors are quiet and calm: faded taupes and creams temper the light and give the room an almost sepia quality, like an old photograph. There's a good rug on the floor, a Bessarabian, which also makes it feel more like a room.

You won't find any seashell knobs on the drawers. Nothing in here is sentimental or cute. The vanity is faced in sturdy beadboard, and the hardware is very basic—just old-fashioned bin pulls, the kind of thing you could get at the local hardware store. The idea is to make the room feel as if no decorator ever touched it. Instead, it just evolved.

The tub is a refurbished antique, which I found in Chicago. I always like to have a table nearby, where you can set down a drink or your cell phone. But I get bored with the usual wood side table, so I'm continually on a search for something different. This rolling metal table fits the bill. It looks like something that might have been used in a factory, and the wheels make it even more convenient. Lighting is crucial to mood, and I always want to be able to dim the lights in a bathroom. The sconces by the tub give off a soft, warm glow. They're modeled after an antique I found in Paris. Here, I had them made in a pewter-y finish to suit the unpretentious nature of the house.

MONTECITO, CALIFORNIA

There are some things that are so magical they are like an expressway to emotion, and for me the handpainted, timeworn blue-and-white tiles you see all over Portugal instantly evoke the romance of another era. When my clients and I decided to build a Portuguese-style house, they became the unifying factor through the rooms. I fell in love with various tiles at the Museu Nacional do Azulejo—the extraordinary tile museum in Lisbon—and had them reproduced. But not so they looked new. I wanted that old pitted quality and an antique-looking glaze. We even broke some, so it would look as though they had been on these walls for years.

In the kitchen, they form a vibrant, geometric backsplash that transports you to another time and place. I found an old French fabric seller's table, topped it with a slab of stone, and used it as an island. The barstool also came from the French flea market and is more of a perch than a chair. Both pieces have their own history and patina, just like the reclaimed French terra-cotta floor tiles, which kept everything on the same level, so to speak. It felt like a kitchen you might see in a Portuguese *quinta*, or country house, right down to the bowls of oranges from the trees in the garden.

ABOVE: The white stucco house, crowned with baroque finials, was modeled on a Portuguese country estate. OPPOSITE: There's a nobility to simplicity, and the kitchen is actually very spare, with simple white woodwork and an eighteenth-century-style hood over the range. I found the antique plates in Lisbon. The huge, beautifully shaped terra-cotta jar probably held olive oil at one time.

The handpainted tiles may be new, but they were deliberately made to look old. The colors are soft and mellow. And that tarnished mirror looks as if it has been here forever. It's all about creating mood.

The Portuguese word for tile, *azulejo*, comes from the Arabic word *az-zulavi*, and there's definitely an Islamic influence that you can trace through the various designs. By the mid-sixteenth-century when its ships were crisscrossing the oceans, Portugal was the richest country in the world and Moorish, Italian, Flemish, and Dutch tiles were just some of the spoils carried home in the holds. The Portuguese people developed such a passion for tile that they started producing their own versions.

They used them in a very distinctive, architectural way—as a kind of wainscot in a room—and I recreated that here. I like that lovely contrast of rough, thick plaster and smooth, cool tile. And it really starts to get interesting when you put multiple patterns together. It becomes almost psychedelic. The intricacy of the design draws you in and you can get lost in the swirls.

Practically nobody was making these kinds of tiles when we did this project, which is why we had to have them specially made. And I couldn't find the right kind of sink, so we had one made, using old, salvaged legs that we refinished. That was the impetus for my own line of kitchen and bath fixtures. It all came about because I could never find what I was envisioning in any store or showroom. When you stand at this sink and look into that mirror, you feel as if you've gone to another country and a quieter, gentler time.

ABOVE: The border tiles act as a proscenium, framing the tub and shower. OPPOSITE: There's a wide, usable surface on the sink, but I also supplemented it with a little Chinese table on the side that can hold more toiletries. I'm always interested in the idea of something mechanical and utilitarian that was modern in its own time, like that telescoping shaving mirror. The antique mirror, from the Paris flea market, has that distressed look I love. And the glass bell on the sconces from Vaughn is partially frosted, so it looks a little smoky, and that gives it a sense of age.

This tile is so graphic it looks almost like op art, or something from the Jazz Age in the 1920s. Actually, this kind of simple patterning has been around for centuries.

The guesthouse is not that big, but all this bold pattern in a small space gives it a sense of luxury and a vivid identity. The colors stay consistent, but the pattern changes from room to room.

In the small kitchen, we turned a traditional checkerboard on a diagonal to animate it. The glaze is super slick, which makes the tile feel very clean and crisp, and the white painted cabinets and the white appliances look brighter against it.

The diagonals in the bathroom are livelier and even harder to do. It took forever to get each piece positioned properly. But the effort was worth it. It totally transforms the room. Bathing in that tub becomes a visual as well as a sensual experience. I'm not sure it would work as well in a big space, where the graphics might become a bit overwhelming. Here, it turned a small, innocuous room into a little jewel. It's a treat to go in and brush your teeth. You can't help smiling.

ABOVE: I like the way the tile runs all the way up behind the open shelves. We installed a farmhouse sink and a refurbished antique stove to give the kitchen a period look. OPPOSITE: Architect Oscar Shamamian designed the great leaded glass window over the tub. It adds another layer of complexity to the design.

PALM SPRINGS, CALIFORNIA

In the harsh light of the desert, every tree, every rock, every bit of scrub is silhouetted against the sun. The landscape is stark and primitive. Any shadow becomes a respite. Houses are built with deep overhangs to shelter the interiors from the sun, and the long, low planes of modernist architecture seem to echo the flat stretches of earth and sky. The world feels as if it has been reduced down to its elements.

There's that same elemental quality to the materials we chose for this kitchen. The American walnut used for the cabinetry has a lovely pattern to the grain. It's the same type of wood that the great furniture maker George Nakashima often used for his free-form tables and benches. He made an ordinary piece of furniture look like sculpture by recognizing the beauty of the material and then letting it speak for itself. No other decoration was necessary on these cabinets. The handles are as simple and unobtrusive as we could make them.

The colors recall the natural colors of the landscape. The tiles on the backsplash have a dusty greenish tint, like the dry, sandy earth outside. There's an island in the center of the room topped with CaesarStone, a manufactured product made primarily of quartz. And the island is a reasonable size, not huge, because I'm not a fan of gigantic islands. When they get too big, preparing a meal can turn into an obstacle course—and you don't want to have to do laps around an island to get to the refrigerator. It makes more sense to organize the island and countertops into separate zones. Here, there's one for prep, one for washing dishes, and one for eating.

Form follows function, and it all looks exceptionally serene. But what makes this kitchen truly special is the art. A large-scale photograph by Thomas Struth hangs on one wall and depicts a jungle scene. It's a virtual diorama of lushness, a sharp contrast to the hot, dry landscape outside. And yet it underscores a point: this house is an oasis in the desert. The courtyard just beyond the kitchen door is planted with trees. Here is your refuge. You can be in the desert and yet sheltered from it.

In the great California tradition, the house is a permeable membrane, open to the outdoors. But the desert outside is hot, so inside, all is coolness. Dark wood absorbs some of the sun's glare. The light is controlled, with a skylight over the island to give you more light just where you need it, as you're preparing the food. I like a gooseneck faucet because it has clean, simple lines. It's also supremely practical—the high spout doesn't get in the way of big pots. FOLLOWING SPREAD: Leo Marmol and Ron Radziner were the architects on this project, and they designed and built the beautiful cabinetry. The backsplash tiles were handmade by Heath Ceramics.

Artwork adds drama and transports you to another place. The photo, by Thomas Struth from his Paradise series, is so green and verdant that just looking at it cools you down. I can't imagine the kitchen without it. All you'd have is a plain, flat wall, and the room would lose that sense of another dimension and another world. Simple, leather-backed wooden stools are pulled up to the breakfast bar.

The dressing room is my homage to Jean-Michel Frank, the great French designer who famously covered the walls of a Paris apartment in parchment, and Luis Barragán, the Mexican architect who seemed to carve rooms out of space and light. It's so simple and reductive, like their work. The elegance is in the discipline. The dressing room is done with just one material—walnut—on the closet doors and the streamlined chest of drawers. You really focus on the beauty of the wood. It envelops you and creates an amazing sense of warmth and richness.

The walnut reappears in the bathroom, where it frames the mirrors and forms the vanity. As a contrast to it, but still in a similar tone, I chose a taupe limestone for the counter and the tub surround. The faucets by Thomas O'Brien for Waterworks were done in a custom bronze finish to keep to the same brown tones. The bath becomes a study in sepia. By limiting the palette to variations on one shade, you create a room that feels unified and calm and restful.

ABOVE LEFT: The rectangular shape of the mirrors and the slim lines of the light fixtures by Philippe Anthonioz repeat themselves and create a rhythm. ABOVE RIGHT: If you look closely, you can see fossils embedded in the stone that encases the tub. OPPOSITE: In the dressing room, even the handles repeat the long rectangle of the drawers and are made of the same walnut. The chest seems to float off the floor, which makes it feel less heavy.

BEVERLY HILLS, CALIFORNIA

Early in my career, I redid this 1950s ranch house for a very supportive client and her husband. We took down walls and completely re-designed the kitchen to turn it into a simplified, shorthand version of something you might find in the English countryside. This was long before the days when everyone was ordering bespoke pine plate racks from companies like Smallbone of Devizes. If we wanted something, we had to make it. And, in any event, this was an Americanized version, with red faux-leather banquettes around the breakfast table. It looked like one of those cheery booths in a diner.

The architect Marc Appleton and I divided the long rectangular room into three bays—the breakfast area, the cooking area, and the butler's pantry. The cabinetry is plain and simple white, and the countertops are dark mahogany. It's a classic look that still manages to be very utilitarian and unpretentious, as if you were walking into a farmhouse. There's a sturdy dhurrie rug on the floor in front of the sink. Pullout wicker baskets for onions and potatoes are tucked into a cubby under the counter, and that's about as fancy as the built-ins get. You don't need a lot of bells and whistles.

The upper cabinets in the foreground hang from the ceiling and have glass doors on both sides, so you can access them from the kitchen or the butler's pantry. That way, they don't block the light but still separate the two areas. The tin ceiling and the schoolhouse light fixtures by Urban Archaeology help create an old-fashioned feeling.

When this house was built, small bathrooms were the order of the day. But we wanted more than just the basics. We wanted a chaise to relax on, a table for your tea. It's a different idea of how to live in your house, and it goes back to an earlier era. I tried to bring in a bit of history with the old-fashioned tiles on the floor and the Edwardian-looking fixtures on the tub, which are by Czech & Speake. A cheval mirror in the Biedermeier style in lovely honey-colored wood adds a lot of personality. It's much more warm and engaging than an ordinary full-length mirror attached to the back of a door. There are no curtains in the room, just wood Venetian blinds. Nothing is fussy. It all has a certain simplicity.

ABOVE: The Greek key design in the floor tiles is done in this funny 1930s green, and we picked up the color in the ticking on the French chaise. We also painted the table in a similar shade of green. The vanity on the right looks like another piece of furniture. OPPOSITE: There's great charm in that little gilt chair by the tub, which feels as if someone pulled it in from another room and never bothered to put it back.

MALLORCA, SPAIN

This island off the eastern coast of Spain may be technically Spanish, but it's one of those places where you see a fascinating mix of cultures. France is nearby, but that's just one influence. Many international travelers pass through every year, and that's been going on for centuries. Palma de Mallorca was once a very wealthy port. I was surprised when someone told me there are more palaces here than there are in Rome.

When I first came to visit, I was captivated by the juxtaposition of the formal and the informal. In historic houses, you see damask curtains and terra-cotta floors. My clients bought a comparatively new house, but they wanted it to feel old, weathered, and quintessentially Mallorcan.

The kitchen we did could have looked much the same, minus a few modern conveniences, 150 years ago. I found a seventeenth-century Hispano-Moroccan tile in Toledo, Spain, and had it copied for the walls. The colors—intense greens and blues and yellows—and the incised pattern add a lot of richness and depth. The cabinets and the island were already there, but we simplified them. I got rid of some of the uppers and replaced them with open shelves. I wanted it to feel like things were a little haphazard, and a shelf or a cabinet was just added when the need arose. And they don't necessarily match, like the different-sized cabinets on either side of the hood. The countertops are made of rustic wood, with a glazed finish.

I found the breakfast table in London at Colefax and Fowler and bought the chairs at auction in California. Sometimes it's less expensive to buy Spanish furniture in London or California than it is to buy it in Spain. Actually, that's often true of antiques. The country of origin will usually hold it in higher value. I had the chairs covered in a kind of Louis XIII fabric by Prelle, a French company that has been around since 1752. It comes with a built-in patina, as if the blue was once bright but has faded over the years. Even the material looks somewhat eroded. It feels almost as if it has been sanded down. To add atmosphere, which doubles as task lighting over the island, I hung English-style lanterns that were made in California. This kitchen is my own version of the Mallorcan mix.

I bought that great big armoire at the flea market in Paris. It holds an immense amount and makes the room feel older. If we had filled up the wall with built-ins, it would have looked too kitchen-y and too new. A seventeenth-century Spanish painting, done on wood, hangs in the living room just beyond and sets an old-world mood. The simple terra-cotta tile floor is typical. I love the coolness in the summer months and the practicality. It never occurred to me to change it.

The open shelves hold primitive jugs and other country pottery. I like the decorative effect of plates hung on the wall and the hood. The Spanish chargers have great character and depth, like mini paintings.

In this guest bathroom, you can see the light touch and the casual charm that runs all the way through the house. I wish I could take credit for the grillwork on the vanity. It's very practical, especially in a place where you get the sea breezes, because it lets the contents of the cupboards breathe. The architect who built this house approximately ten years ago also designed the vanity, and he did a very nice job. I like the softening effect of the curve at one end and the convenient open shelves, which make it easy to grab a towel. The top is made out of white marble, with a nice old-fashioned silhouette to the backsplash. The sink was lovely. I didn't need to touch any of this.

My most noticeable contribution is the large black-framed mirror and the pictures that surround it. That strong black outline is a very Spanish idea, and I repeated it on the picture frames. The pictures themselves are probably English. The designs are cut out of floral chintz and then glued onto the paper. It must have been a very charming pastime for a young lady, or at least I like to think of it that way.

Arranging pictures is an art in itself, but you always want it to look artless. The two little English sconces on either side of the mirror somehow make the composition feel less formal. I always like some sort of chair in a bathroom, and I found that ebonized bench at the Paris flea market. It's covered in a Henry Calvin fabric. The rug is a traditional Mallorcan stripe and has been made in exactly the same way for centuries.

BRENTWOOD, CALIFORNIA

A great bathroom can have a transformative effect on the way you start your day, not to mention your whole perception of a house. I had a vision of a pavilion in a garden, which could take the master suite in this New England–style house to a whole new level. So we appropriated a completely ordinary space formerly used as an office and rebuilt it to create this big, beautiful shared bathroom that's part garden folly and part Malmaison.

The first thing you see as you walk in the door is the oeil-de-boeuf window, which should cue you in to the classical origins of the room. It's all about proportion and symmetry. The volume is unusually generous, with a ceiling that soars and a pair of French doors that open to a sequestered garden planted with only white roses. The clients love white, and the room is predominantly white, which always feels clean and pure. Two white pedestal sinks—reclaimed from the Plaza Hotel—flank the window, and each has a glass shelf floating above it, with a beveled glass mirror masking a medicine cabinet. All these fixtures are very traditional and make me think longingly of those grand old hotels where I've stayed in Paris and London. Those hotel baths have a simple elegance, which I find very reassuring, somehow.

Of course, there is a trade-off when you choose a pedestal sink—you lose the potential for storage underneath—so I set a neoclassical chest in between them to hold toiletries. It's made of dark wood, which sets off a nice contrast with all that white. And something interesting happens when you bring a real piece of furniture into a bathroom: it becomes less utilitarian and more cozy. In this case, though, it's really the French Empire table in the center that transforms your whole concept of the room. This is the kind of table you might see in a foyer, and I've used it the same way I would there—as a repository for books and some eye-catching art. An old English lantern hangs above it and marks the center of the space.

There are no curtains. They're not necessary, and the room looks more reductive this way, and stronger. Your eye goes to the architecture and the view. You never lose sight of those roses.

A tall terra-cotta pot is the focal point of a long, narrow garden that runs between the screening room, on the left, and the main house, which is off to the right. The buildings are small in scale, to look like a New England village.

These pedestal sinks are ipso facto classical—they stand on columns. The floor is painted with a wash, so you can still see the grain of the wood through the pattern. It reminds me of Sweden, and it relates to the Gustavian cabinet in the dressing room in the foreground. A Turkish runner in front of the sinks provides some warmth where you would stand. When you're walking on a rug with bare feet, I want it to feel very flat. No shag carpets, where you might pick up bits of yarn between wet toes.

There's something very old-school about this kitchen, and it's not just the old schoolhouse-style light fixtures. There's a familiar quality to each and every one of the materials. Take those simple square white tiles on the backsplash, for example. We recognize them from so many rooms in our past. Same with the traditional white-painted cabinets with glass doors and the butcher-block countertops. You could plunk just about any American down in this kitchen, and he or she would immediately feel comfortable getting out the frying pan and making some bacon and eggs.

It's very reassuring to walk into a space and feel as if you've been there before, even if it was only at the movies or in your imagination. This is what I think of as a Connecticut country kitchen, but it's been streamlined to work for a modern family. There are no cute little accessories cluttering up the space. The only things out on the countertops are the tools you need for cooking and an old portable TV.

The one detail that makes the kitchen unique is that scene of a lighthouse, painted on a set of tiles and placed in the natural focal point over the range. It's a more modern take on the old blue-and-white Delft tiles, also painted with pictures, that would have traditionally held that spot. The lighthouse with the clouds rolling by is a scene that holds memories for the clients, and it makes this kitchen theirs. It's a good reminder that you always want to include something that's personal and important to you in any room. It adds life.

The professional-style Viking range is a sleek contrast to the old painted table, topped with a new, extra-thick layer of butcher block. The vintage child's chair is convenient for little helpers. Two coffeemakers mean you can make decaf and regular coffee at the same time.

RESOURCES

APPLIANCES

BlueStar
29 E. 19th Street
New York, NY 10003
T: 212-955-0500
www.bluestarcooking.com

Miele
150 East 58th Street, 9th Floor
New York, NY 10155
T: 800-843-7231
www.mieleusa.com

Sub-Zero/Wolf
50 East 58th Street, 5th Floor
New York, NY 10155
T: 212-207-9223
www.subzero.com

Viking Range Corporation
5151 Commerce Drive
Baldwin Park, CA 91706
T: 626-338-3800
www.vikingrange.com

ARCHITECTS

Appleton & Associates Inc.
1556 17th Street
Santa Monica, CA 90404
T: 310-828-0430
www.appleton-architects.com

Ferguson & Shamamian
Architects
270 Lafayette Street, Suite 300
New York, NY 10012
T: 212-941-8088
www.fergusonshamamian.com

ForestStudio
332 Forest Avenue, Suite 4
Laguna Beach, California 92651
T: 949-497-0202

G.P. Schafer Architect, PLLC
270 Lafayette Street, Suite 1302
New York, NY 10012
T: 212-965-1355
www.gpschafer.com

Kovac Architects, Inc.
2330 Pontius Avenue, Suite 202
Los Angeles, CA 90064
T: 310-575-3621
www.kovacarchitects.com

Marmol Radziner
12210 Nebraska Avenue
Los Angeles, CA 90025
T: 310-826-6222
www.marmol-radziner.com

Nancy Peacock Inc.
2048B Ualakaa Street #B
Honolulu, HI 96822
Tel: 808-947-0047

OZ Architecture
3003 Larimer Street
Denver, CO 80205
T: 303-861-5704
www.ozarch.com

Rios Clementi Hale Studios
639 North Larchmont Boulevard
Los Angeles, CA 90004
T: 323-785-1800
www.rios.com

Tichenor & Thorp Architects
8730 Wilshire Boulevard,
Penthouse
Beverly Hills, CA 90211
T: 310-358-8444
www.tichenorandthorp.com

CABINETS

Arclinea Los Angeles
8687 Melrose Avenue B121
West Hollywood, CA 90069
T: 310-657-5391
www.arclinealosangeles.com

Boffi USA
150 East 58th Street, Suite 801
New York, NY 10055
www.boffi.com

Bulthaup
158 Wooster Street
New York, NY 10012
T: 212-966-7183
http://www.en.bulthaup.com

DPC Woodwork Inc
5714 West Pico Boulevard
Los Angeles, CA 90019
T: 323-935-4828

HARDWARE

Carter Hardware, Inc.
153 North Robertson Boulevard
Beverly Hills, CA 90211
T: 310-657-1940

E.R. Butler & Co.
By Appointment
55 Prince Street
New York, NY 10012
www.erbutler.com

Merit Metal Products
242 Valley Road
Warrington, PA 18976
T: 215-343-2500
www.mcritmctal.com

The Nanz Company
20 Vandam Street
New York, NY 10013
T: 212-367-7000
www.nanz.com

P.E. Guerin
23 Jane St.
New York, NY 10014
T: 212-243-5270
www.peguerin.com

Rocky Mountain Hardware
1030 Airport Way
Hailey, ID 83333
T: 888-788-2013
www.rockymountainhardware.com

Sun Valley Bronze
323 Lewis Street, Suite A
Ketchum, ID 83340
T: 208-788-3631
www.sunvalleybronze.com

LIGHTING

Ann-Morris Antiques, Inc.
239 East 60th Street
New York, NY 10022
T: 212-755-3308

Chameleon Fine Lighting
223 East 59th Street
New York, NY 10022
T: 212-355-6300
www.chameleon59.com

Holly Hunt
150 East 58th Street,
New York NY 10055
T: 212-826-4184

Paul Ferrante
8464 Melrose Place,
Los Angeles, CA 90069
T: 323-653-4142
www.paulferrante.com

PLUMBING

Kallista
7 East 18th Street
New York, NY 10003
T: 212-529-2800
www.kallista.com

The Kohler Store
100 Merchandise Mart
Chicago, IL 60654
T: 312-755-2510
www.thekohlerstore.com

Lefroy Brooks
163 Merchandise Mart
Chicago, IL 60654
T: 312-755-0776
www.lefroybrooks.com

Salvage One
1840 W. Hubbard
Chicago, IL 60622
T: 312-733-0098
www.salvageone.com

Urban Archaeology
239 East 58th Street
New York, NY 10022
T: 212-371-4646
www.urbanarchaeology.com

Waterworks
215 E 58th Street
New York, NY 10022
T: 212-371-9266
www.waterworks.com

The Water Monopoly
16/18 Lonsdale Road
London NW6 6RD
T: 44 20 7624 2636
www.watermonopoly.com

STONE, TILE & WOOD

Ann Sacks Tile & Stone
7 East 18th Street
New York, NY 10003
T: 212-529-2800
www.annsacks.com

Baba Wood
4380 Alston Chapel Road
Pittsboro, NC 273112
T: 919-542-6920
www.baba.com

Country Floors
15 East 16th Street
New York, NY 10003
T: 212-627-8300
www.countryfloors.com

Exquisite Surfaces
150 East 58th Street, 9th Floor
New York, NY 10155
T: 212-355-7990
www.xsurfaces.com

Heath Ceramics
7525 Beverly Boulevard
Los Angeles, CA 90036
T: 323-965-0800
www.heathceramics.com

Lascaux Tile Company
By Appointment
T: 323-939-6039
www.lascauxtile.net

Mosaic House Inc.
32 West 22nd Street
New York, NY 10010
T: 212-414-2525

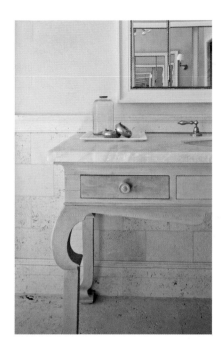

Walker Zanger, Inc.
37 E. 20th Street
New York, NY 10003
T: 212-844-3000
www.walkerzanger.com

PAINT & PAINTERS

Benjamin Moore
200 Lexington Avenue, Suite 714
New York, NY 10016
T: 212-684-2001
www.benjaminmoore.com

Donald Kauffman Color
191 9th Avenue
New York, NY 10011
T: 212-243-5266
www.donaldkaufmancolor.com

Farrow & Ball
979 Third Avenue, Suite 1519
New York, NY
T: 212-752-5544
us.farrow-ball.com

Pierre Finkelstein Decorative
Painting
20 West 20th Street, Suite 1009
New York, NY 10011
T: 212-328-9278
www.fauxbrushes.com

Pratt & Lambert
1956 3rd Avenue
New York, NY, 10029
T: 212-427-6505
www.prattandlambert.com

Steve Beattie Painting, Inc
By Appointment
Brentwood, CA
T: 310-454-1786

Tim Flemming
By Appointment
Chicago, IL
T: 773-484-3080

WALLCOVERINGS

Charles Edwards Antiques Ltd.
582 Kings Road
London SW6 2DY
T: 44-20-7736-8490
www.charlesedwards.com

Collier Webb
120 Fulham Road
London SW3 6HU
T: 44-20-7373-8888
www.collierwebb.com

Elizabeth Dow
8525 Melrose Avenue
West Hollywood, CA 90069
T: 310-315-3028
www.ElizabethDow.com

de Gournay
112 Old Church Street,
Chelsea, London SW3 6EP
T: 44-20-7352-9988
www.degournay.com

Gracie
979 Third Avenue, Suite 1411
New York, NY 10022
T: 212-924-6816
www.graciestudio.com

Jasper
8525 Melrose Avenue
West Hollywood, CA 90069
T: 310-315-3028
www.michaelsmithinc.com

Remains Lighting
213 East 59th Street
New York, NY 10022
T: 212-675-8051
www.remains.com

Vaughan Designs Inc
979 Third Avenue, Suite 1511
New York NY 10022
T: 212-319-7070

ACKNOWLEDGMENTS

I cannot begin to express my heartfelt thanks and gratitude to the amazing individuals at Rizzoli. Many thanks to publisher Charles Miers and editor Kathleen Jayes for their unwavering commitment and excellence in this our third venture together.

It has been a pleasure to collaborate again with the wonderfully talented writer Christine Pittel. Thank you for capturing my thoughts so eloquently once again.

I thank my friend of eighteen years and gifted collaborator Mark Matuszak.

Longtime friend Margaret Russell has been immensely supportive. Thank you for your keen insights and above all your friendship.

Many thanks to Doug Turshen and Steve Turner for masterfully organizing these projects. Your dedication to this project is very much appreciated.

To the numerous unbelievably talented photographers that have captured the very essence and quality of each room. I thank you.

Thank you to Robert Stone for stepping in and orchestrating all of the sections together beautifully.

This book would have been impossible without the generous support and assistance of my amazing clients. Also a very big thank you to my amazing design team for always making it seem so effortless.

Thank you to James for your continual support and encouragement.

CREDITS

Endpapers: Courtesy of
Ann Sacks

Billy Cunningham: 164, 168-171

Brian Doben: 120-123

Courtesy of Kallista: 220-222

Francois Halard: 2, 9-17, 19-25, 29, 77-79, 80 left, 81-83, 87, 178-183, 223 bottom

Grey Crawford: 6, 18, 27-28, 37, 40-42, 45-49, 61-65, 75-76, 80 right, 86 left, 91, 106, 107, 140-148, 153-161, 172-177, 197-199, 202-203, 223 top

Henry Bourne: 108-111, 137-139, 163, 165-167, 190-193, back cover

www.JohnEllisPhoto.com: 84

Lisa Romerein: 31-35, 86 right, 103, 106 left, 194-195

Michael Mundy: front cover, 57-59, 112-119, 130-135, 204-207, 214-219

Michel Arnaud: 99, 101

© Mona Kuhn: 8, 72, 150

Pieter Estersohn / Art Department: 129

Scott Frances / August: 66-71, 92-97, 104-105, 185-189, 200-201

Simon Upton: 50-55, 125-127

Simon Upton © The World of Interiors: 208-213

Thomas Loof / TruckArchive.com: 38-39, 43

William Abranowicz / Art + Commerce: 88-89